MYSTICISM AND THE EASTERN CHURCH

MYSTICISM AND THE EASTERN CHURCH

BY

NICHOLAS ARSENIEW

LECTURER IN THE RUSSIAN LANGUAGE IN THE UNIVERSITY OF KÖNIGSBERG

Translated from the German by ARTHUR CHAMBERS

With a Preface by
PROFESSOR FRIEDRICH HEILER

Introduction by
EVELYN UNDERHILL

LONDON
STUDENT CHRISTIAN MOVEMENT
32 RUSSELL SQUARE, W.C. I
1926

First published April 1926

PRINTED IN GREAT BRITAIN BY
THE EDINBURGH PRESS, 9 AND 11 YOUNG STREET, EDINBURGH

CONTENTS

CONTENTS

PREFACE TO THE GERMAN EDITION*

INQUIRY into the truth and Christianity of mysticism continues to vex theological science. Deeply-rooted prejudices not only bar the way to knowledge of its nature and value, but even interfere with the mere examination of its manifestations. The existence of certain historical connections between Christian and pre-Christian mysticism blind many theologians to the unmistakable individuality of Christian mysticism, which has its roots in the glad message of the incarnate and risen Christ and manifests itself in a life of burning love. Sâdhu Sundar Singh is a brilliant exponent of a Christian mysticism whose source is faith in the living Christ and which proves conformity to its Lord and Master by preaching its Gospel and by loving the brethren as He taught us to do. The present volume from the pen of a Russian scholar brings forcefully before our eyes the wonderful power of Christian mysticism to affirm life and glorify the world. Nicholas Arseniew, who here speaks for the first time in an individual work to the German reader, is particularly well qualified for his task. He not only commands an astonishing knowledge of the mystical literature of both the East and the West, such as no Western scholar, apart from the brilliant

* *Ostkirche und Mystik*, Reinhardt, Munich, 1925.

English investigator, Miss Evelyn Underhill, can show; but, as a sensitive son of Russia and a devout and inspired member of the Eastern Church, he enjoys a special mystical *charisma*, an intimate contact with the world of mystical experience that only few cultured Westerners can claim. This rare combination of comprehensive erudition and ardent piety makes him the correct interpreter of the mysterious message which Christian mysticism has for us, and also of that potent and intimate piety which the Eastern Church conceals behind the shimmering brilliance of its liturgical pomp.

Concerning the origin and varied personal career of Arseniew the following may be mentioned here. On his father's side he comes of an ancient Russian family of the nobility. The founder of this family was the Tartar chief, Arslan Mursa Tschelibey, who in 1389 entered the service of the Grand Prince Dimitrij Joannovitch of Moscow and received in baptism the name Prokopius. He gave to his son the name of Arsenius, and from him the family name derives. Arseniew's mother, *née* Schenschin, traces her origin to a Tartar chieftain who settled in Russia in the fifteenth century. Nicholas Arseniew was born in Stockholm on the 28th of May 1888, being the son of the Russian Counsellor of Legation, Sergius Arseniew, who later held the office of Russian Minister in various European countries. Nicholas Arseniew's school and university education took place in Moscow, where he passed the State examination in 1910. He completed his training at the German Universities of Munich,

Freiburg and Berlin, from 1910 to 1912. In March
1914 he became lecturer (*Privat-Dozent*) at the
University of Moscow in History of West European
Literature. After the outbreak of war he gave up
his academical activities for work with the Russian
Red Cross. After 1916 he lectured in Moscow
on the History of Romance Literature and the
History of Religion. After the Bolsheviks had seized
the power of government, he suffered the fate
of many members of the teaching profession
and was twice imprisoned. On his release from
prison he was, in the autumn of 1918, elected
Professor of Romance Philology in the University
of Saratof. In February 1920 the newly-founded
Chair of Comparative Religious History at the same
University was offered to him. But two months
later he was compelled to leave his native country, as
the Soviet authorities were again upon his track.
Like many of his compatriots he found refuge in
Germany, where in the autumn of 1920 he took
over the Lectureship of Russian Language in the
University of Königsberg and for some time lectured
also in Religious History in the Latvian University
of Riga. Arseniew also taught in the Russian
Hochschule in Berlin.

In his early youth Nicholas Arseniew made himself intimately acquainted with the Bible and with
the mystical literature of the Eastern and Western
Churches. Accordingly, all his scientific work was
also directed from the outset to the sphere of
mysticism. In his numerous publications in Russian,
which are enumerated here, he treats lovingly and
sensitively the problems of mysticism from the

9

historical, psychological, and philosophical points of view.

W iskanijach absoljutnagu Boga (In Search of the Absolute Divinity), Moscow, 1910, 42 pp.

Plač po umiraješema bogu (The Lament for the Dying God) in the "Ethnographical Outlook," Moscow, 1912, and published separately, 36 pp.

Platonism ljubwi i krassoty w literaturje epochi Wosroždenija (The Platonic doctrine of the Eros and of Beauty in the Literature of the Renaissance) in "Journal of the Ministry for Popular Education," St Petersburg, 1913, 103 pp.

Pessimism Giacomo Leopardi (The Pessimism of Giacomo Leopardi), in the "Journal of the Minis. of Pop. Educ.," St Petersburg, 1914, and separately, 80 pp.

Golos ljubwi, nieskoljko akkordov is mističeskoj poesij Srednich Wekov (The Voice of Love, Echoes from the Mystical Poetry of the Middle Ages), Moscow, 1916, 16 pp.

Misticism i lirika, is oblasti mističeskoj poesij Srednich Wekov (Mysticism and Lyricism in the Mystical Poetry of the Middle Ages), "Journal of the Minis. of Pop. Educ.," St Petersburg, 1917, and separately, 16 pp.

Otkrovenija božestwennej ljubwi Julianij is Norwiča (The Revelations of Divine Love of Julian of Norwich), Moscow, 1918, 31 pp.

Wnutrennjaja piesnj duši, is oblasti mistiki (The Inward Song of the Soul in the Sphere of Mysticism), in "Russian Thought," Sofia, 1921, 14 pp. (in German in the *Archiv für Religionswissenschaf*, xxii.).

PREFACE TO THE GERMAN EDITION

Žažda podlinnago bytija, pessimism i mistika (The Thirst for
True Being, Pessimism and Mysticism), Berlin, 1922,
230 pp.

*Obras straždušťago Christa w religiosnych perežiwanijach
Srednich Wekov* (The Figure of the Suffering Christ
in the Religious Experiences of the Middle Ages), in
Trudy russkich učjonych sa granitzej (Work of Russian
Scholars Abroad), II, Berlin, 1923, 14 pp.

Tainstwo Ewcharistij w žisni Cerkwi (The Sacrament of the
Eucharist in the Life of the Church), in *Problemy
russkago religiosnago ssosnanija* (Problems of Russian
Religious Philosophy), Berlin, 1924, 25 pp.

There have appeared in German : *The Russian Soul and
the Spirit of the Eastern Church*, Lecture given in
Darmstadt ·in the *Leuchter* (Otto Reichel, Darmstadt), 1924, pp. 187-234.

Dostoievski's Struggle for God, 1925, 28 pp. ; *The Resurrection from the Dead*, in the *Leuchter*, 1925, pp. 219-248;
The Eastern Church, in *Sammlung Göschen*. No. 918,
1926, 104 pp.

In the present work Arseniew makes his rich
knowledge and profound grasp of mysticism access-
ible to German readers. In the first part he introduces us to the " Spirit of the Eastern Church,"
unknown to most outsiders, and acquaints us with
his own religious position—unbroken faith in the
risen Christ and in the Easter joy which springs
from this faith. From this standpoint he succeeds
in throwing light upon that aspect of Christian
mysticism which always remained incomprehensible

to the dry rationalism and profane worldliness of Western scholars, "The Transfiguration of the World and of Life in Mysticism."

May Arseniew's work help to reveal the inexhaustible power of the mysticism of the living Christ ! May it also help to further in the religious world of Germany understanding and appreciation of the Eastern Church, which indeed is not a Church of rigid formalism and meaningless ritual, but a treasure-house and source of living religious power ! May it also reawaken admiration for the depths of piety of the national soul of Russia, for the extermination of which her materialistic rulers have worked in vain !

FRIEDRICH HEILER.

THE FEAST OF THE SLAV
   APOSTLES SAINT CYRILLUS
      AND SAINT METHODIUS.
  MARBURG, 7th July 1924.

INTRODUCTORY NOTE

I HAVE been asked to add a few words to the Preface in which my friend Professor Heiler so admirably introduces this profound and beautiful study of the spirituality of the Orthodox Church. It is a book for which English students of religion have long been waiting, conscious that Eastern Christianity had much to reveal to them, could they find a guide to its living realities. In Professor Arseniew we have such a guide ; learned, widely read in the religious literature of the world, and a devoted lover of the mysticism of his Church. He writes of it with a contagious enthusiasm, a vivid realism, which make of this brief essay a work of spiritual as well as academic worth.

So long as our view of Christian mysticism is based only on a study of the Catholic and Protestant mystics of the west, it will inevitably be lop-sided and incomplete. Even such glimpses into the hidden life of the Eastern Church as Cassian's Dialogues or the Greek Fathers give us, warn us that there another type of spiritual culture grew up ; having its own particular riches, its own gifts to make to the total consciousness of the Church of Christ. But difficulties of language, and the formidably ceremonial exterior which is all that Orthodox Christianity shows to the uninitiated, have hitherto blocked the way to any deep understanding of its mystical experience : an experience which has developed without a break from that characterising

Primitive Christianity, and sometimes contrasts with, sometimes completes and supports our own.

Yet there are times when ceremonial can and does reveal the living heart beneath its complicated garments. It happened to me once that being in Rome I went on Easter Eve to the Church of the Uniat Greeks; a body which retains almost intact the Orthodox ritual and spirit. The tiny church was crammed with people, and amongst them walked a magnificent and bearded ecclesiastic, whose dress would not have been out of place at the Council of Nicæa. He was followed by two little boys carrying a large washing-basket which was full of daffodils, primroses, and wild cyclamen: and he was throwing the flowers in handfuls over the people, crying in Greek " Christ is Risen ! " It was the bringing-in of Easter Day.

Now that scene, with its flowery spring-like feeling, its exultant certitude of a risen and triumphant life, its Christo-centric ecstasy linked closely with the renewal of the natural world, strikes the note which meets us again and again in Professor Arseniew's work. He shows us a mysticism, essentially Johannine in type, which we might call both Catholic and Evangelical : a religious realism so ardent and so objective, that beside it the mild ethical piety of Liberal Protestantism seems thin and prosaic. This mysticism is centred upon the Resurrection, and the continued presence in the world of the Exalted Christ as giver of Eternal Life. It finds its perfect institutional expression in the Eucharist ; and the wonderful Communion prayers of the Eastern liturgies are alone enough to convince us of the profoundly mystical sense in which this sacrament is understood.

Here, in this "discovery of the inward in the outward"—this weaving together of the things of spirit and of sense—Orthodox spirituality has, it seems to me, much to teach the modern West. The type of Christianity which most appeals to us tends more and more to be predominantly terrestrial and utilitarian in outlook ; is slow to understand the true meaning and worth of its own religious institutions ; is ever ready to set up a false opposition between ceremony and spirituality, between the body and the soul of the Church. Here, on the other hand, as in the mysticism of St Francis, a profound supernaturalism is linked to a lovely naturalism. The visible world in its entirety is, or may be, a manifestation of the glory of God; and the Christian message of hope extends beyond man to the whole created universe, which is destined to be redeemed and transfigured by the life-giving Spirit of Christ. Already it is through the transfiguration of its simplest elements, that the very life of God is communicated to men. Thus the Eucharist, as the focal point of Christian worship, whilst losing none of its personal and life-giving character, takes on a cosmic meaning. It witnesses to the ultimate transfiguration of the things of earth by an invasion of supernatural power. It points beyond the here and now to a transubstantiation of the whole material order ; a veritable "bringing in of the Kingdom of God."

EVELYN UNDERHILL.

MYSTICISM AND THE EASTERN CHURCH

I

THE SPIRIT OF THE EASTERN CHURCH

CHAPTER I

EARLY CHRISTIAN FAITH IN THE RESURRECTION

THE joy of the resurrection—that is the key-note of the Eastern Church's whole outlook upon the world. "Let the heavens rejoice in seemly way, and let the earth be glad; let the whole world give praise, both the visible and the invisible: Christ is risen, joy eternal! Now is all filled with light: the Heaven, the earth and the under-world, let therefore all creation praise Christ's resurrection which is its firm foundation! . . . We give praise for the slaying of death, the destruction of Hades, the dawn of a new life, life eternal,"—thus the Eastern Church sings in its Easter hymns.

This same mood, this same basic refrain pervades also the whole preaching of primitive Christianity. The fundamental meaning of this preaching, so far as we can apprehend it, is indeed the message of the revelation and of the triumph of eternal life. "For the life was manifested, and we have seen it, and bear witness, and shew unto you that eternal life, which was with the Father, and was manifested unto us." "And if Christ be not risen, then is our preaching vain, and your faith is also vain. . . . But now is Christ risen from the dead, and become the first-fruits of them that slept!"[1] Herein lies the source of that mighty note of joy and triumph which is so characteristic of early Christian psychology. "And this is the victory that overcometh the world, even our faith." "Rejoice evermore . . . in everything give thanks."[2]

Let us allow ourselves a cursory glance. According to the testimony of the Acts of the Apostles the whole message originally entrusted to the apostles was the preaching of Christ's resurrection. "Whom God hath raised up, having loosed the pains of death : because it was not possible that He should be holden of it . . . whereof we are all witnesses"—thus runs the first sermon of the apostles (that of Peter) to the people. The apostles were persecuted by the priests and Sadducees because they "preached through Jesus the resurrection from the dead." "And with great power gave the apostles witness of the resurrection of the Lord Jesus," we read a little later. "Him God raised up the third day, and shewed Him openly ; Not to all the people, but unto witnesses chosen before of God, even to us, who did eat and drink with Him after He rose from the dead"—Peter preaches in the house of Cornelius.[3] Faith in the revelation of the divine, eternal life in the person of Jesus is the essence of the whole outlook, the whole preaching of Paul. And in this respect he feels no contradiction between his preaching and

that of the other apostles : " Therefore whether it
were I or they, so we preach, and so ye believed." [4]
The fifteenth chapter of the first Epistle to the
Corinthians and the writings of John are the most
emphatic and ringing testimony of this jubilant
early Christian message of the revelation of eternal
life.   The words of Jesus in the fourth Gospel
concerning " eternal life " of which they partake
who believe in the Son ; the " living water " which
He will give to these and which in them " shall
be a well of water springing up into everlasting
life " ; the " bread of life " of which " if any man
eat, he shall live for ever " ; the promise, " The
hour is coming, and now is, when the dead shall
hear the voice of the Son of God : and they that
hear shall live " ; and, perhaps of special weight, His
words : " I am the resurrection and the life . . ." ;
again, the solemn words of The Revelation : " I am
the first and the last ; I am He that liveth,
and was dead ; and, behold, I am alive for evermore,
Amen ; and have the keys of hell and of death " ;
and, again : " Be thou faithful unto death, and I
will give thee a crown of life " ; and lastly, the
triumphant cry of Paul : " It is sown in corruption ;
it is raised in incorruption : it is sown in weakness ;
it is raised in power. . . .   O death, where is thy
sting ?   O grave, where is thy victory ? "—all these
words express that jubilant exaltation of the spirit,
that sublime hope, founded upon belief in the
resurrection, in which early Christianity lived and
moved, and whereby it grew and waxed strong and
conquered the world.[5]   Out of this faith were born
the first preaching and the earliest hopes of the

primitive Church ; without this faith in the resurrection of Jesus and the victory of life, there would have been no primitive Church and no Christianity. And this faith also remains the essential, inspiring force of Christianity through the times that followed. The inscriptions in the Catacombs exhale this joy, this confidence in eternal life. " Thou livest, live in peace, in the glory of our Lord " (ζήσῃς, *vivis, vivas, vive in pace, in gloria Dei et in pace Domini nostri*). The portion of the departed is the " portion of life " (τὸ τῆς ζωῆς μέρος), " He goeth to the living God " (πρὸς τὸν ζῶντα θεόν).[6] The Christian martyrs are filled with the same faith, the same inspiration. " I seek Him who died for us ; I desire Him who for us rose again," writes Ignatius of Antioch to the Romans.[7] " I thank Thee," prays the aged Polycarp at the stake, " for that Thou hast made me worthy this day and at this hour to partake among the number of Thy witnesses of the cup of Thy Christ, for the resurrection unto eternal life with body and soul, in the incorruptibility of the Holy Spirit. . . ."[8] All these prayers are full of thanks for the gift of eternal life bestowed through the Son of God. " Thou gavest me spiritual food and drink and eternal life through Thy servant (Son) "—we read in the eucharistic prayer of the *Didache*.[9] The same tones of joy over the revelation of eternal life ring through the Odes of Solomon. The following words are placed in the mouth of the risen Christ :

" . . . They have sought Me, that set their hope upon Me, because I live. And I am risen, am among them and speak through their mouth. . . .

" And I have not sunk, though men thought it of Me.

" Hell hath seen Me and was compassionate.

" And death hath permitted Me to return, and many with Me.

" I have become vinegar and gall to him (death), and I descended with him (death) to the lowest depths (of Hell).

" I allowed My feet and head to droop for they could not bear My face.

" And I gathered an assemblage of the living among his (death's) dead and spake with them with living lips. . . .

"But I heard their voice and wrote My name upon their head. For they are free men and belong unto Me, Hallelujah." [10]

With His victory over death is bound up in the Odes, as also in Paul and all the preaching of primitive Christianity, the promise of eternal life and of resurrection for those who believe on His name. " Redemption is sure through Him and His abundance is everlasting life ! " [11] " I have put on immortality through His name," says the believer, " and have laid aside mortality through His goodness." [12] " I drank and became drunk with the living, deathless water—and the Lord renewed me in His raiment and possessed me in His light." [13] The faithful " have been saved by the living water that endureth for ever." [14]

We find ourselves in an atmosphere like that of

John's inspirations; here hovers the spirit of the fourth Gospel and of the " Revelation " of John.

This mood of exalted joy crystallised into an outlook upon the world. This outlook is already present in its completeness in the early Christian preaching [15]; its theoretical formulation and evolution and its further religious fixation came about during the following centuries—in the writings of the Fathers and in religious practice.

A religious realism is thoroughly characteristic already of the earliest Christianity : the Incarnation, the Passion, and the Resurrection of the Son of God are not illusion, not deception, as the Docetists and other Gnostics taught, but reality. But if this be so, then the flesh also, which the Son of God put on and in which He rose again, has not been cast aside ; it also has a part in the Life, for it took into itself the germ of immortality. " Now is Christ risen from the dead, and become the first-fruits of them that slept. . . . For as in Adam all die, even so in Christ shall all be made alive." [16] Hence we have the rehabilitation of the matter and of the flesh : the body is not a " sepulchre " (the platonic $\sigma\hat{\omega}\mu\alpha$-$\sigma\hat{\eta}\mu\alpha$), not a " prison " of the soul, but " a temple of the Holy Ghost." Hence the ardent expectation of " the redemption of our body," the belief in the resurrection of the body, the inspired preaching of this doctrine which appeared so paradoxical and offensive to the scholars of antiquity. This is the reason also why this doctrine was so strongly emphasised by the Christian apologists, even those who were most strongly under the influence of the contemporary philosophy and who tried to force the religious experience of Christianity into the incongruous and narrow frame of this popular philosophy at the cost of a partial dilution and weakening of its religious peculiarity. But they could not renounce the resurrection of the flesh, however seriously this might contradict the philosophical fashion, the basic principles of the one-sided platonic " spiritualism " ; for this resurrection of the whole man was the essence of the religious hopes of Christianity, and these hopes were indivisibly bound up with the resurrection in the flesh and the glorification of the risen Lord and Master. God the omnipotent is the Creator of the whole world, Creator also of the flesh. There are no limits to His power and dominion. The Christian consciousness could not therefore be reconciled to the existing state of the world " lying in wickedness," could not regard this state as final. It believed in the ultimate complete victory of life and abolition of death, release from the dominion of sin and corruption, the glorification of all existing things, of the whole cosmos, of all creation in the kingdom of eternal life. There will be " A new Heaven and a new Earth." We know that " the whole creation groaneth and travaileth in pain together until now." " For the creature was made subject to vanity, not willingly . . . in hope, because the creature itself also shall be delivered from the bondage of corruption into the glorious liberty of the children of God " . . . " that God may be all in all." [17] These hopes of Paul remained fundamental and definitive for the religious life and faith of Christianity through the times that followed ; this joy and confidence in the resurrection became the basis also of the Eastern Church's outlook—nay more, they constitute its very essence, its most intimate, deepest, most vital nature.

Let us bring before our minds in a few examples the further expression of this religious realism, this jubilant confidence, these exalted expectations in the life of the Church. In the recently discovered, remarkable monument of the primitive Church's outlook during the second half of the second century (about 160 to 170, in the judgment of the editor, Karl Schmidt)—the so-called " Epistola apostolorum "—the author lays particular stress upon the doctrine of the resurrection. Christ is truly risen in the flesh—this receives especial emphasis. " We heard Him and touched Him, after He was risen from the dead," [18] say the apostles. And again : " We therefore touched Him (and convinced ourselves) that He was indeed arisen in the flesh," [19] etc. From the fact of the incarnation of the Son of God and His resurrection in the flesh follows the promise of our resurrection also, and of our share in His glory. " For therefore am I come in the flesh," says Jesus to the apostles, " that ye may arise in your flesh in the second birth in a garment that shall not be cast aside." [20] " What is now sunk shall rise again and what is diseased shall be made whole, that in this My Father may be praised. As He hath done unto Me, even so will I do unto you and unto all that believe on Me." [21]

Irenæus fervently champions the resurrection of the body, the rehabilitation of the matter, against the Gnostics. For how can the body be lost which

24

in the sacrament of the Lord's Supper has partaken of the body and blood of Christ! " Our bodies which have taken into them the Eucharist are no longer perishable, but have hope of the resurrection . . . they will rise in their time." [22] Christ is the new, the second Adam. " He hath raised fallen man," and has become flesh, " to give proof of the resurrection of the body." [23] Redemption is " casting off of death " and the gift of God is eternal life.[24] About A.D. 200 Tertullian pleads with special weight and power the high worth of the body and the doctrine of the resurrection. " *Fiducia Christianorum—resurrectio mortuorum* "—" The faith of Christians is the resurrection of the dead," are the opening words of his famous " *De resurrectione carnis*." Tertullian develops an exhaustive argument, full of temperament and conviction. The creation of man in God's image does not refer only to the soul, but also to the body, for the body also has assumed the image of the incarnate Christ (*jam tunc imaginem induens Christi futuri in carne*). As the body strives and suffers together with the soul, together with the soul it must also be glorified. Together with the soul it partakes of the sacraments, feeds upon the body and blood of Christ ; is a " sister " of Christ's flesh (" *Christi sui sororem* ").[25]

These same ideas and inspirations flood the writings of the great Fathers of the Christian East. In Athanasius they are concentrated in a particularly emphatic and outspoken manner, like rays of light in a burning-glass, and constitute a potent philosophy. For herein are to be found the essence and the deepest roots of his whole piety ; he feels himself constantly gripped afresh by the great fact of the redemption from death, corruption, and sin, and of the renewal of man, and his spirit soars ever afresh in joyful confidence. Especially well known are his splendid words : " God hath become man that we might be made divine." [26] " Yea, verily," he writes in an Easter letter to his flock at Alexandria, " it is a thing rich in joy, this triumphant victory over death, and our immortality (won) by that body of the Lord. For as He is risen, so likewise shall our resurrection come to pass, and His body, which remained untouched by corruption, becometh without doubt the source of our incorruptibility." [27] Therefore " All creation rejoices, oh my brethren ; and every living breath, in the words of the Psalmist, sings praise unto the Lord who has destroyed our enemies. For our salvation is accomplished." [28] This joy in the resurrection, this Easter joy, persists even in sorrow and tribulation ; unquenchable, it flames up in persecution, exile, and oppression.[29] For death is even now conquered, " set aside," " exterminated," " destroyed " [30] ; death has no further terrors for us. " For, as through man death had won power over man, so through the incarnation of the Word of God the destruction of death and the resurrection of the body are come to pass. . . . For we no longer die as men damned, but await, as risen men, the common resurrection." [31] This same philosophy of redemption and resurrection is also to be found, more systematically developed, in Gregory of Nyssa. " God united Himself with our nature," he writes, " in order that our nature might be made divine through union with God, delivered from the hands of death and freed from bondage to the enemy : for His resurrection from the dead is for mortal man a beginning of the resurrection unto eternal life." [32]

Two fourth-century Fathers of the Church, John Chrysostom and Ephraem Syrus, who have both, especially Chrysostom, left an indelible trail upon the life of the Eastern Church, preach with particular fire, force, and depth the joy of the resurrection, the victory of life over death and the coming glorification of the flesh also. Chrysostom has written an exhaustive commentary on the passages of St Paul dealing with this subject. In his homily, " Concerning the Resurrection of the Dead," he takes as his starting-point Paul's words in the second Epistle to the Corinthians : " Not for that we would be unclothed, but clothed upon, that mortality might be swallowed up of life." " These," says Chrysostom, " are words by which the slanderers of the nature of the body, the impeachers of our flesh, are completely overthrown. By His words : ' We do groan . . . not for that we would be unclothed,' Paul seeks to warn us positively against the belief that he despises the body as something evil, the cause of sin, an enemy and adversary. . . . What he means to say is roughly this : We do not wish to cast aside the body, but corruption ; not the flesh, but death. The body is one thing, corruption another ; the body is one thing, death another . . . the body is corruptible, but not corruption ; the body is mortal, but is not death. Rather is the body a work of God, while corruption and death, on the other hand, first came into being through sin. That which is foreign to me, says Paul, that I desire to cast off, not that which is my own. What is foreign to us, however, is not the body but corruptibility. Therefore he says: 'Not for that we would be unclothed'—*i.e.*, of the body—'but clothed upon'—with incorruptibility upon the body, . . . 'so that mortality may be swallowed up by life!' Thus he speaks in no way of destruction of the body but of destruction of death and corruptibility." [33]

Chrysostom also preaches in ringing tones this faith in the future resurrection of the body in his exposition of the fifteenth chapter of the first Epistle to the Corinthians: "What! The dead not rise! If they rise not wherefore is Christ risen? Wherefore is He come? Wherefore hath He put on the flesh, if He had not the intention to raise the flesh? For He Himself had no need of it, but did this for our sakes. . . ." [34]

But potentially this glorification is now granted, though still in a hidden form. It is this, as Chrysostom points out, that Paul teaches: "Not of a glory first beginning (ἔσεσδαι), but of a glory to be made manifest (ἀποκαλυφθῆναι), exactly as though it were already an established fact though as yet veiled." [35]

These hopes of a coming resurrection and glorification of the body are also presented, with no less inspiration and fire, in the hymns of Ephraem Syrus. "The will of his Creator," he says of the body, "shall gather together his dust, shall renew it and make of it the temple of glory; the body

28

shall lead his companion, the soul, into the bridal chamber and there comfort her ; and the body filled with sorrow in Hades shall rejoice, and the body that hath despaired shall give praise, for his redemption, and that over which the foolish despaired shall receive great mercy. The feet, which were bound, shall leap in Paradise . . . the eyes, which were closed, shall behold the fount of all light. The mouth, which was dumb, shall be opened. . . . And the body, which was corrupted, shall shine in glory." [36] "Although Adam liveth no more, he was created by Thee, that he might live ; therefore shall his temple be renewed by Thee, which is now become dust. . . . An overpowering spectacle it was when Thy radiant majesty descended into the dark dust to create the splendid image. This last (the incarnation) was much higher than the first (the creation of Adam), for Thou didst not only create the dust, but didst put it on Thyself. . . . Make glad the body through the soul, but restore the body to the soul, that they may both rejoice in that after the separation they are again united. Let the soul approach that she may enter into her house and be at peace in her dwelling and her light shine therein." [37] "The first-born (the Son of God) was clothed with a body ; He used it as a veil for His splendour. The immortal Bridegroom shone in this garment. May the garments of the guests become like unto His ! May your bodies shine—which are your garments ! " [38]

This rejoicing of the Fathers of the Church over the resurrection of Christ and over His, and consequently also our, victory over death, finds perhaps its noblest expression in that wonderful sermon of Chrysostom which is up to the present day solemnly read on Easter night in the Eastern Church : " . . . Enter ye all into the joy of your Lord ; the first and the last receive their reward ; rich and poor rejoice together, abstinent and heedless honour the day. Ye who have fasted and ye who have not fasted rejoice together to-day ! Let none bewail his poverty, for the riches of all have appeared. Let none sorrow over his sins, for forgiveness shineth forth from the grave. Let none fear death, for the death of the Saviour hath redeemed us. He hath stamped out death who was embraced by death, He hath made hell captive who went down into hell. He hath troubled it after it had tasted His body. . . . O death, where is thy sting ? O grave, where is thy victory ? Christ is risen and the demons are fallen. Christ is risen and the angels rejoice. Christ is risen and life liveth. Christ is risen and of the dead there is none left in the grave : for Christ, risen from the dead, is become the first-fruit among them that sleep there ! To Him be honour and dominion for ever and ever ! "

What force of faith and what courage are implied in this statement : " Christ is risen and of the dead there is none left in the grave " ! True, it is contrary to daily experience. But in this belief we are touching on the realm of eternity, of eternal life, where the boundaries between the present and the transcendent future vanish.[39]

These hopes, this faith, this jubilation—these constitute the key-note of the life and outlook of the Eastern Christian Church.

CHAPTER II

Easter Joy in the Eastern Liturgy

As we have seen, hope, faith, and jubilation are characteristics of the spirit of primitive Christianity; they are common to all forms of Christianity, not the exclusive property of the Eastern Church. And yet this much may be said: in the Eastern Church they have remained decisive and dominant; joy in the resurrection, joyous yearning of the soul towards the glory to come, a mystically contemplative anticipation of the glory of eternal life. Attempts are sometimes made to draw comparisons between the piety of the Roman Catholic Church and that of the Eastern Church; it is said that in the centre of the religious life of the former stands the suffering Christ, in the centre of the latter the risen Christ. This is a contrast which must not be pressed. For the Roman Catholic Church, too, the Saviour is the risen Christ, and the Eastern Church also contemplates with fervent devotion the Passion of the incarnate Christ (cf. the impressive ritual of Holy Week). But in a certain restricted sense this contrast can be maintained. The Eastern Church concentrates her whole fervour upon the glory of the risen Lord. The radiance of His transfigured life even now lights up the world and life. The primitive, joyful, mystical and, at the same time, eschatological realism here appears in all its force and significance. Death *is* at the present moment already conquered, the relentless cosmic laws are suppressed, the power of corruption and sin are destroyed, the whole world and our bodies also are *in spe*, *in potentia*, already partakers of eternal life. This spirit, this triumph, this joy of victory pervade, for example, all the resounding anthems of the Eastern Church's year.

Nor does the Eastern Church, any more than the Western, shut her eyes to the transience, the shadowiness of our life, our earthly blossoming, or to the pain of death, the separation of the soul from the body and from all a man loves on earth, or to the terrors of death and the horror of corruption.

" O woe ! " thus runs the impressive dirge of the Church, " What strife the soul endures, when she parts from the body ! Alas, how she weeps and there is no one to comfort her."

" I weep and moan when I think of death and see beauty made in the image of God lying in the grave ugly and shapeless. . . ."

" Verily is this a mystery of death ; how the soul is parted by force from the body, how she is loosed by God's will from the companionship of natural union. . . ." [40]

The fear of death rings in these words, terror of the last death struggle. All earthly things are transitory, illusory and vain.

" What earthly joy is without sorrow ? " it goes on. " What glory endures on earth ? . . ."

" Men, why are we anxious ? The way we tread

is short.   Life is smoke, vapour, dust and ashes, brief it seems and passes quickly ! "

" Where is love of the world ?   Where the vision of temporal things ?   Where are gold and silver ? Where the throng of servants and fame ?   All is dust, ashes, shadow !   But let us draw near and cry to the everlasting King : Lord vouchsafe to those that are parted from us Thy eternal blessings." [41]

For there is a redemption !   High above these cries of grief swell and soar the mighty, all-compelling notes of deliverance and glory—joy in the victory of life, in the resurrection from the dead.

" Christ is risen, the first-fruit of them that sleep " —in various forms, but with ever-renewed power this rings out from these hymns.   And yet this bold message of the resurrection is inseparably linked with the message of the Cross and the martyrdom of the Saviour ; by death He hath overcome death. This spirit pervades the songs of the *Oktoichos* (the root-stock of the Church's hymns for the year).[42]   Just a few examples :

" Nailed to the Cross of Thine Own will, O compassionate One ; laid in the grave as dead, O Life-giver, Thou hast destroyed the dominion of death, O mighty One, by Thy death.   For before Thee the gates of Hades yawned open, but Thou hast awakened with Thee those that were dead since the beginning of time, Thou the one Lover of Mankind ! "

" King, hanging from the Cross, O only mighty One, Thou hast moved all creation ; but laid in the grave, Thou hast awakened the dwellers in the grave, pouring upon mankind immortality and life :

therefore we glorify Thee, praising Thy rising after three days ! "

" The women came to the grave in the early morning and seeing the vision of the angel were afraid. From the grave life shone forth : the wonder of it filled them with fear. Therefore they went away and proclaimed to the apostles the resurrection : From hell Christ snatched its prey, Christ alone powerful and mighty, and awakened all that rotted in the grave."

" Life-bringing, fairer than Paradise, and, in truth, more radiant than any earthly pomp, appeared, O Christ, Thy grave, the source of our resurrection," [43] etc.

We see His resurrection from the dead is the pledge of our resurrection also, nay more—it *is* already our resurrection, our victory also over death :

" Thou hast destroyed the dominion of death, O mighty One, by Thy death," " Thou hast awakened with Thee those that were dead since the beginning of time," " Thou hast awakened the dwellers in the grave, pouring upon mankind immortality and life," . . . " Thou hast delivered the dead and, rising after three days, hast clothed the dead with immortality." " He is risen, making empty the graves ! Behold the changeless Changer of corruption ! " " He hath made the dead to live ! " " To-day are death and hell robbed of their prey, but mankind is clothed in immortality " ; " The dead that death had swallowed up death hath restored ; for the destructive dominion of hell was itself destroyed when Thou, O Lord, didst rise from the grave ! " [44]

This exuberant joy is manifested in ever-changing means of expression, for there is already a sharing of His resurrection, already is there mystic experience, mystic realisation of the glory to come. In His person the whole human race (symbolised by its father, Adam) is already, at the present time, potentially risen from the dead and made divine : " Adam falls and is crushed ; disappointed of old in his hope of divinity, yet he rises, made divine by union with the Word, and wins through suffering immunity from suffering ; upon the throne he is glorified as the Son, sitting beside the Father and the Spirit ! " [45]

And—as we have already seen—it is not man alone who is affected by the redemption and the joy of victory ; with the joy over our resurrection is linked also joy over the redemption of the whole world, over the ending of the dominion of corruption, over the redemption of all creation and the dawn of the kingdom of life. And the eye of the spirit gazes fervently out towards the glory to come—that " splendid freedom of the children of God," of which all creation shall partake. The resurrection is thus an event of cosmic significance, and the world, equally with man, is thereby already permeated by the radiance of the celestial glory, although as yet in hidden form, and has attained to a new and high worth ; for it has already taken into itself the germ of immortality. Christ, so sings the Eastern Church, is " risen as God from the grave in glory and hath thereby raised the whole world with Him," " giving His life for the world," He has " filled the whole world, the whole creation, with light," He has

35

" illumined with the radiance of His coming and brightened by His Cross the ends of the world," He has " made the earthly one with the heavenly." [46] " O wonder ! How did the life of the All taste death ? Only that it might lighten the world." [47]

Therefore is the whole world, the whole creation, summoned to rejoice and sing praises to the Lord : " Rejoice, O creation, and blossom like the lily ! For Christ is risen from the dead as God ! O death, where is thy sting ? O hell, where is thy victory ? " [48] " Let the heavens rejoice and the earthly things shout with joy, for the Lord hath worked power with His arm : He hath trodden death under foot by His death." [49] " All creation rejoicing singeth to Thee with the prophets the song of victory." [50] " The ends of the world rejoice in Thy awakening from the dead." [51]

As we have already said, this exaltation reaches its climax on Easter Night and in the preparation for the festival of the Resurrection in the services of Holy Week. Throughout Holy Week the last days of the Saviour upon earth are vividly re-enacted—His way of sorrow, the Last Supper, then the story of His Passion, death and burial. There is an atmosphere of solemnity which reaches far beyond the interior of the Church, and is not merely connected with the religious service (which, incidentally, from the Monday of Holy Week fills the half of each day), but dominates life—even in the family, in the home. In this stillness of Holy Week one hears the footsteps of the Lord walking towards Golgotha—a solemn, earnest mood of contrition, abasement and deepest emotion. And at last, on the eve of Good Friday, come the " twelve Gospels "—evoking, re-enacting the Passion of our Lord! The accounts of the Passion are read aloud. Trembling with reverential awe, the Church sings : " To-day hangs upon the Cross, He who hung the earth above the waters ; the King of the angels is crowned with thorns ; He who clothes the heavens with clouds is clothed in mockery with purple. . . . The Bridegroom of the Church is nailed with nails, the Son of the virgin is pierced with the lance. We adore Thy Passion, O Christ. Show unto us also Thy glorious resurrection ! "

And still louder, in the wondrously solemn service of the night between Good Friday and Easter Eve, we hear tones of joyous confidence and hope blending with the dirges and the great Burial Psalm (119), which are read over the Christ stretched upon the bier. " The honourable Joseph, after he had taken down Thy holy body from the Cross, and had swathed it in a clean linen cloth, and covered it with sweet-smelling ointments, laid it in a new grave." The angel that appeared at the sepulchre cried to the women bearing spices : " Spices are for the dead, but Christ knew not corruption." Then follow alternately verses from the " Psalm of Death " (119), and verses concerning the laying of Christ in the grave and His victory over the grave :

" Blessed are they that live without blame, who journey in the law of the Lord."

" Thou, the Life, wert laid in the grave, O Christ ; and the hosts of the angels shuddered, praising Thy humility."

37

" Blessed are they that keep His testimony, that seek Him with their whole heart ! "

" O Life, how canst Thou perish ? How canst Thou dwell in the grave ? But Thou destroyest the dominion of death and raisest the dead out of the abyss of hell."

Blending in wonderful harmony, the rhythmic Old Testament Psalm, which is the Eastern Church's farewell for the guidance of the departed soul, and the vibrant, fervent cry of the Church, trembling with awe before the grave of the Saviour, continually answer one another :

" For whosoever wandereth along His way doeth no evil."

" We glorify Thee, O Jesu, King, and we adore Thy burial and Thy Passion whereby Thou hast redeemed us from corruption."

" Thou hast commanded to keep diligently Thy commandments."

" Thou that didst determine the measure of the earth, dwellest to-day in a narrow grave, O Jesu, Ruler of All, that raisest the dead from the graves."

" Oh, that my life may keep Thy laws in all earnestness."

" O Jesu, my Christ, King over all, seeking what didst Thou come down to them that are in hell ? Verily in order to redeem mankind ! "

" If I look only upon Thy laws I shall not be defiled."

" The Lord of all is looked upon as dead and is laid in a new grave, He that hath emptied the graves of the dead. . . ."

The notes of mourning and the ringing tones of

confidence intermingle. This mood grows and swells as Easter draws near. It reaches one of its climaxes during the day service of Saturday. The church is draped in black, the celebrants still wear vestments of mourning, the prayers of penitence still continue ; but already there hovers over everything a presentiment, a breath of the resurrection.

After many long passages from the Old Testament, dealing with the New Covenant and the joy of the redemption by God's hand and might, and the hope of deliverance from death, the song of the three men in the fiery furnace is solemnly chanted in the centre of the church—again, a symbol of the resurrection of the Saviour—and after each verse of the song the choir breaks in with the powerful refrain : " Praise the Lord, and glorify Him to all eternity ! " The fervour increases and soars aloft. After the short Gospel comes a moment of supreme exaltation for the congregation. A trio of boys' voices cry the words of the Psalm : " Arise, O Lord, and judge the earth, for Thou reignest unto eternity ! " And with a passionate uplifting of the heart the congregation reply : " Arise, O Lord, and judge the earth, for Thou shalt inherit in all nations ! " And again the three boys' voices sing—this time already words from the New Testament concerning the New Covenant : " Christ our Passover, slain yet alive, the Lamb of God that taketh upon Himself the sins of the world." And once more the congregation breaks in with the appeal : " Arise, O Lord, and judge the earth. . . ." All the new hope, the whole essence of the faith, is concentrated in this cry. It is a fervent cry of the soul, a common appeal of the whole Church ;

it is, as it were, a wrestling with God. He must rise! For without His resurrection our faith is vain, our salvation vain. It is an ardent, passionate reiteration of the tremendous, overwhelming message. The cry ever grows and swells, ever grows and swells the tension, the Church's exaltation; it is a kind of spiritual crescendo, a great soul symphony, the pure voices of the boys singing the words of promised joy, and the urgent, unceasing, tirelessly reiterated appeal, the Church's prayer at the graveside of her Lord. "The angel cried to her that was filled with grace," the boys' voices sing, "pure virgin, rejoice, for thy Son is risen after three days from the grave." And the choir replies: "Rise, O Lord, and judge the earth, for Thou shalt inherit in all nations!" And, finally, the clear voices of the boys raise yet again the jubilant cry: "Rise, O Lord, and judge the earth, for Thou reignest unto eternity!" Then the deacon emerges from the altar-room, already wearing the white and silver vestments of rejoicing, and proclaims the gospel of the resurrection: the women came to the sepulchre, but the stone was rolled away, and the angel said to them: "Why seek ye the Living among the dead? He is risen! Go and tell His disciples!"

And at last comes Easter night, with its glad tone of jubilation. On the stroke of midnight, while all the candles blaze into light—a sea of candles surging in the hands of the congregation—there ring at last from the mouth of the priest and deacon the long-expected, eagerly-awaited words of joy: "Thy resurrection, O Christ and Saviour, is sung by the angels

in the heavens. Let us too on earth sing Thy praise."
And from a thousand throats swells and soars the
triumph song of Easter night : "Christ is risen from
the dead, after He overcame death by death and
gave life to them that were in the grave." And
over and over again is repeated this short verse,
sanctified by its tremendous import and the custom
of centuries as the best, the dearest, the most
familiar, the universally current, cherished expression
of the Church's exultant Easter joy. And inter-
mingled with this follow in succession the splendid
hymns and Easter canons of John of Damascus.

"It is the day of the resurrection, let us be filled
with light, O people. Passover of the Lord, Passover! For from death to life, from earth to heaven,
hath Christ, our God, led us, who sing the song of
victory."

"Come let us drink of the new drink that springeth
forth, not from the barren stone but from the grave
of the Saviour, a spring of life incorruptible. . . ."

"The women bearing spices . . . cried one to
another : O friends, come let us anoint with sweet-
smelling spices the buried body of the Life-giver,
of Him that hath raised the flesh of the fallen Adam,
that lay in the grave."

"We sing the slaying of death, the destruction of
hell, the dawn of a new life, life eternal. . . ."

"To-day every creature rejoiceth and shouteth
with joy : for Christ is risen and hell is bound !
. . . The holy Paschal Lamb hath to-day revealed
Himself to us, the new Passover filled with holiness,
the mystic Passover, the pure Passover, the great
Passover, the Passover of the faithful, Who hath

opened for us the gates of Paradise, the Passover adored of all the faithful ! "

" . . . Passover ! Let us embrace one another with joy, O Passover ! This is our redemption from pain ; for shining forth from the grave as from a palace, Christ hath filled the women with joy, saying : tell the disciples."

" It is the day of the resurrection ; let us be filled with joy and embrace one another ; even unto them that hate us let us say : O brethren, we forgive one another for the sake of the resurrection, and so we cry : Christ is risen from the dead, overcoming death through His death. . . ."

This is the heart, the focal point, the vital nerve of the whole piety of the Eastern Church—joy in the risen living Lord, joy in His glorification and life ; for His life is also our life, transfigured, eternal.

Not only in the past was this joyful faith the centre of the Eastern Church's inner life, nor does it now live only in the Church's cult and ritual. A faith living only in ritual, or in the past, in archæology or the conservation of tradition could not be a living faith. But in the Eastern Church faith in the resurrection and Easter joy is a living faith. From it have sprung the noblest evidences of Russia's spiritual life (the lives and works of her saints, her religious art and, as we shall see later, the outlook of such a man as Dostoievski). But there is more than this ; this Easter faith has shown itself to be a tremendous and uninterrupted living force, by which men may find joy in suffering and death, and which has called forth recent martyrs for the Christian faith. Under the Bolshevist yoke many thousands have suffered torture and death for their Christian faith (8000 clergy alone); racked, some even torn to pieces, shot, burned, imprisoned. And they died cheerfully. And this persecution, the most appalling tyranny of impious power that the world has ever seen, could not kill their Easter joy, or make the many who remained true to Him, or rather found their faith in Him, deny their risen and glorified Lord, the victor over the power of hell. There awoke in the hearts of these people a spirit akin to that of primitive Christianity which had its source in the same faith. Eloquent testimony of this is furnished by a letter written by Benjamin, Metropolitan of Petersburg, shortly before he was shot by the Bolsheviks—it exhales the very spirit of that of Ignatius of Antioch to the Romans before he was thrown to the beasts in the arena.[52] This same spirit is also illustrated by the following story, which has been very widely told in Russia. In a large public assembly hall (the Polytechnic Museum) in Moscow, a public lecture was given by Comrade Lunatscharsky, the Bolshevist Commissary for Popular Education, attacking the "obsolete faith." This faith, he said, was a product of the capitalist class, but was now completely overthrown; its nullity was easy to prove. The address seemed very successful and the lecturer was so pleased with his own eloquence that, feeling complete confidence in himself, he brought it to an end by inviting a discussion of his theme, but with the stipulation that no speaker was to occupy more than five minutes. Anyone who wished to address the meeting was to give him his name. There came forward a young priest with a close cropped beard, of homely appearance, shy and awkward—a typical village priest. Lunatscharsky looked down at him scornfully: "Remember, not more than five minutes." "Yes, certainly. I shan't take long." The priest then mounted the platform, turned to the audience, and said: "Brothers and sisters: *Christôs wôskresse!*—Christ is risen!" (The solemn Easter greeting exchanged by all on Easter night.) As one man the great audience answered: "*Woistinu wôskresse!*—Verily He is risen!" (The usual reply.) "I have finished. I have no more to say." The meeting was at once closed. All Comrade Lunatscharsky's flowery eloquence availed him nothing.[53]

This story is characteristic; for in these confident words of the Easter greeting "Christ is risen! Yes, verily He is risen!" lies the whole essence of the Eastern Church's faith.

CHAPTER III

Asceticism and Transfiguration

But this is no " magic " life, produced from without, no mere externally acquired redemption. It must be won by the sharing of His path of the Cross, His struggle. He who wishes to share His glorified life must be crucified with Him. The old, sinful man must gradually die away. The first step along this path, the all-pervading key-note, the starting-point and, at the same time, the deepest foundation is a feeling of unqualified contrition. " Where shall I begin repentance for my wicked life ? " These opening words of the " Canon of Repentance " of Andreas of Crete are characteristic of this spiritual state.[54] " Wallowing in the depths of sin, I cry unto the unfathomable depths of Thy mercy." " Give me tears, O Christ, to wash away the stains of my heart." " Open to me the gates of repentance (μετάνοια), O Life-giver." And so it goes on, ever increasing in force through the songs of the Church (particularly during Lent), the liturgical prayers, the lives and teaching of her great Saints.

But it is no mere lament over personal wickedness that is required, but also a stubborn struggle, an active defence, an " unseen battle " against evil sinful thoughts, as we find laid down in the pre-

45

cepts of the *Philokalia* (Russian *Dobrotolubije, i.e.,*
" Love of spiritual beauty ")—that famous mystico-
ascetic chrestomathy of the Eastern Church, covering eleven centuries. There are various stages of
this inward struggle, the first being that against
thoughts of the sins of the flesh. The flesh must be
subjugated, curbed, made obedient. For the flesh
wages war against the soul, rebels against the Spirit
of God. Here we have the full solemn and forceful
expression of the ethical (but not metaphysical)
dualism that is so fundamentally important for
the whole Christian morality. A stern, relentless
struggle is waged by these Eastern Fathers for the
mastery of the soul over the flesh by means of its
subjugation, its humiliation. The further, higher
stages of the inward struggle are concerned with
the sins of the spirit—anger, the spirit of despond-
ency, and pride. Indeed, sinful thoughts are
like a countless army assaulting and beleaguering
man from every side. Therefore, the highest
achievement is to maintain that " purity of the
spirit," which is the only true " fruit " of the soul,
and without which all external activity is vain.[55]
Not mere outward putting on of virtue, but " purification of the spirit—that is perfection ! " cries
Makarius.[56] Therein is to be found that inward
" silence " of the spirit, that aloofness from the
clamour of the passions, that silent, rapt concentra-
tion upon God, accompanied, however, by ceaseless
inward " spiritual " prayer, which is conveyed to the
mystics of the Eastern Church by the words : " I
sleep but my heart keeps vigil." [57] The early
Fathers have wonderful things to tell us of this

inward "silence"! "It is a ceaseless prayer to Jesus, a sweet repose of the spirit unbroken by inward stress, a certain wonderful state that comes from union with Jesus," writes Hesychius of Jerusalem.[58] But, as we see, it is not Quietism, quite the contrary; the "silence" of the heart must be accompanied by a ceaseless, active, upward striving of the soul towards God—that is the essential feature of all this inward experience. And it must be accompanied by great "spiritual sobriety," [59] a mistrust of excess of feeling, even in religious experience; searching, honest self-analysis, fear of spiritual "deception." This is the spirit exhaled by all the maxims of the *Philokalia*. Gregorius Sinaita, for instance, writes concerning the danger of self-deception: "Be watchful and heedful, lover of God. If in thy labour thou seest any light or fire, within thee or without, or any shape—Christ's, for example, or that of one of His angels or any other—accept it not; set it aside lest thou suffer harm." We must not allow the power of the imagination to prevail, but must guard ourselves against its images and illusions. "When thou feelest thy spirit drawn upwards, as it were, by an invisible power, trust it not and allow not thy soul to be drawn away, but force it to its work!" That of which we can still harbour doubt comes, not from God, but from the enemy. That which is really from God comes suddenly, unexpectedly and irresistibly. "Very often thou thinkest it to be spiritual joy, and it is merely sensuality roused by the enemy; but the spiritually experienced knoweth it." [60]

47

Alone, and relying on his own powers, man cannot distinguish the dangers, still less withstand them! "The (human) spirit cannot, alone and unaided, overcome the illusions of the demons: nor should it attempt so to do." [61] In the deepest depths, in the abysses of the soul, even of such as are apparently most pure and holy, there lurks the "serpent," who poisons the depths of the spiritual life, and man is powerless to cast him out or kill him. His mind is taken captive and made a "slave of sin." "Every human being, whether Jew or Greek, loves purity, but cannot become pure," writes Makarius of Egypt. Not otherwise is victory over this serpent, hiding in the inmost recesses, possible, "save with the help of Him Who was crucified for us. He is the Way, the Life, the Truth, the Gate." [62] And all the other Fathers say the same. Let us fight against disease of the soul "by calling unceasingly upon our Lord Jesus Christ, for without Him we can do nothing!" cries Hesychius of Jerusalem.[63] Real cleansing of the heart is possible only through Jesus, through the help of grace. And the more a man increases in grace, the more conscious he becomes of his weakness and unworthiness. Therefore, upon the heights to which this path of heart-cleansing leads, there shines the crown of all virtues—humility ($\tau\alpha\pi\epsilon\iota\nu\circ\phi\rho\circ\sigma\acute{\nu}\nu\eta$).

Astonishing things are told of the depth of humility attained by these Fathers of the Eastern Church, these expounders of the Christian life. I will take at random a characteristic story from the old *Book of the Fathers* ($\pi\alpha\tau\epsilon\rho\iota\kappa\acute{\circ}\nu$) of the Egyptian desert —a story of the great saint, Abbot Sisoe.

When, after a long life of spiritual struggle and endeavour, he was nearing his end, his face was suddenly lit as by the sun, and he cried to the Fathers gathered round him : " See, there comes Abbot Antonius ! " And in spirit he gazed upon the hosts of glorified saints, who approached him one by one, and the radiance of his face steadily increased. At last one of the Fathers asked him, " With whom dost thou speak, Abbot ? " and he answered them : " Angels are come to fetch me and I am begging them to grant me yet a little while that I may do penance." The Fathers said to him : " Thou hast no need of penance, Abbot." And he answered : " Verily I say unto you, I have not so much as begun my repentance." And then they all understood that he was perfect.[64]

" For what is perfection ($\dot{\eta}\ \tau\epsilon\lambda\epsilon\iota\acute{o}\tau\eta s$) ? " asks Isaac the Syrian ; and he answers : " Depths of humility " ($\beta\acute{a}\theta os\ \tau a\pi\epsilon\iota\nu\acute{\omega}\sigma\epsilon\omega s$).[65]   And this is how he describes the humble : " The humble man dare not even pray to God to ask anything of Him, and does not know for what he shall pray ; but he merely holds all his feelings mute in the expectation of grace and favour that shall be bestowed upon him by the countenance of the adorable Majesty." [66]

A whole philosophy of humility is developed by Abbot Dorotheus, a great saint of the 6th-7th centuries. " Perfect humility," he says, " proceedeth from the keeping of the commandments. When there is much fruit on the tree, the branches are bowed down by the fruit ; but the branch upon which there is no fruit striveth upwards and groweth straight. There are trees also which bear

D

no fruit while their branches grow upwards. But if a stone be taken and made fast to the branch, bending it downward, the branch will bear fruit. So is it also with the soul; when it humbleth itself it beareth fruit, and the more fruit it beareth the more humble it becometh. The nearer, therefore, the saints approach to God, the more sinful they see themselves to be. Thus Abraham, when he saw God, called himself 'dust and ashes'; and Isaiah, when he looked upon God's sublimity, cried: 'sinful and unclean that I am.'" [67]

As we have seen, this is no shallow, naturalistic optimism. The depths of our depravity and sin are keenly and deeply felt. Contrition, penance, and repentance are called for; an unremitting, stern struggle, ceaseless striving, supreme spiritual effort and activity. And at the same time man feels himself wholly incapable of maintaining this "unseen struggle" alone, of accomplishing anything alone—without grace! He is sinful and weak, poor and naked—what can he do? Only groan from the depths of the abyss and cry for help. And yet "cleansing of the heart" is required of him! That is a logical antinomy, yet its elements—utmost spiritual activity and consciousness of his own complete weakness and poverty, that he can accomplish nothing without grace—are indissolubly, inseparably bound up one with the other. They are mutually dependent, both fundamental constituents of the "life in the spirit" and without them this higher life cannot be. Nor can they be weighed and measured one against the other. One cannot say: so much grace and so much effort;

grace here, effort there. This is a single process of life wherein in a manner indefinable and beyond the reach of external juridical formulæ, the freely-granted divine power, mysterious and life-giving, links itself with the apogee of human spiritual endeavour, itself, however, a fruit of grace. For what can man do alone ?—" Wallowing in the depths of sin I cry unto the unfathomable depths of Thy mercy ! " [68]

Let us turn back to obtain a fuller picture of the spiritual path ! " To the humble is grace given." From the sharing of Christ's crucifixion, from the painful struggle and cleansing process, from the repudiation of self springs joy. On the heights of spiritual growth, where humility shines, where sinful thoughts are conquered and the heart ever more purified—there for the quickened sight the whole creation, to the unpurified once a temptation and a stumbling-block, is transfigured and ennobled. This is the account given, for instance, by John Climax (one of the sternest teachers of the ascetic life) of this glorious consummation of purity of heart : " I know a man who, when he saw a woman of unusual beauty, praised the Creator for her. The sight of her lit within him the love of God and from his eyes gushed a flood of tears. And wondrous was it to behold how that which would have wrought the undoing of another became for him in super-natural manner a crown of victory. If such a man in like cases be always capable of such feelings and such conduct, he hath already partaken of incorruptibility, even before the general resurrection." [69] The whole world then becomes filled with beauty and meaning. Thus, for St Antony the whole visible created

nature is his book and lies open before him whenever he wishes to read God's word.[70] At this supreme stage the flame of love grows ever more intense, and love itself grows ever more perfect, and there develops that of which another great penitent and saint speaks—" a kindling of the heart for all creation —for mankind, the birds, the animals, the demons, the whole creature. And whenever he thinks of them or contemplates them, tears pour from his eyes, because of the strong sympathy which possesses his heart. And his heart feels itself touched and possessed, and he cannot endure to see or hear a creature suffer any hurt, even the slightest pain." [71] As a living commentary to these words we have the stories of some of the Fathers of the Syrian deserts— their sympathy and compassion, which extended even to the wild animals, the obedience which the animals showed to them, and their power over the animals. Similar stories are told also of the Western saints—foremost among them being St Francis of Assisi—and of a number of great Russian teachers and exemplars of the spiritual life : Sergius of Radonesch, Stephen of Perm, the venerable Seraphim. And there is no cause for surprise in this. " When a man attaineth to purity, all things become subject unto him, as unto Adam in Paradise before the fall ! " [72]

Echoes of similar instances of love pouring itself out over all created things, echoes of this mysticism of the Christian Fathers of the East, reverberate through what are perhaps the finest mystical pages of all Russian literature—old Zosima's counsel in the *Brothers Karamasov*. " Brethren, fear not the wickedness of man," we read here. " Love man even in his sin, for that is a love like the love of God, the highest form of love on earth. Love all God's creation, the whole universe, and each grain of sand. Love every leaflet, every ray of God's light; love the beasts, love the plants, love every creature. When you love every creature you will understand the mystery of God in created things. . . ." And out of this develops the state of ecstasy of love, side by side with stern sobriety of spirit : " Be moderate, learn to recognise the suitable hour. When thou art alone, pray. Love to throw thyself upon the earth and to kiss it. Kiss the earth and love unceasingly, insatiably ; love all, love everything ; seek this ecstasy and this abundance. Sprinkle the earth with the tears of thy joy and love these thy tears. Nor be ashamed of this ecstasy but treasure it, for it is a gift from God, a great gift, not granted to many but only to the chosen."

Not only in literature, however, but also on the summits of the religious life of the Russian people, we find this consciousness of a mystic transfiguration of the world, of a mystic joy in the beauty of God, which to the enlightened eye is radiated by all creation. I will only mention one unique little work which reveals quite unexpectedly wonderful depths in the religious life of the Russian people : " *The Confessions of a Pilgrim to his Spiritual Father* " (*Otkrovennye raskasy strannika duchovnomu otzu swojemu*). It dates from the middle of last century and was printed in Kasan in 1883 from a manuscript found in the possession of an old monk of Athos. They are the life confessions of a simple man of the peasant class. Having a withered hand, he was unfit for work. But he could read, and he read voraciously the precepts of the *Philokalia*. He had lost all his kinsfolk and also his small possessions in a fire, after which he set out on a pilgrimage from shrine to shrine, wandering from Siberia to Southern Russia and even to the Holy Land. The precepts of the *Philokalia* regarding unremitting inward "spiritual prayer" sank deep into his heart. And through this unceasing "spiritual prayer" he experienced supreme joy in the deepest solitude—in his forest hut, where he halted to spend a winter, or, again, as he wandered on, far from human habitation. And all nature around him was transfigured by the flood of this overwhelming joy. All creatures testify to him " of the love of God for man, and all things yearn towards and sing the praise of God. And I understood from this what in the *Dobrotolubie* (*Philokalia*) is called, ' Understanding of the words of creation.' And I saw how man may converse with God's creatures." [73] Here we detect an echo of the spirit of the early mystics.

CHAPTER IV

The Sacrament of Sacraments:
The Great Communion.

In the lives of the great saints the bounds confining fallen nature were already to some extent passed. But more than this—in the Church's whole life of grace, especially in the sacraments, there is to be found a glorification of earthly existence through the penetration of the divine actuality. And the consummation of this blending of the two worlds is the Sacrament of Sacraments—the Lord's Supper.

The founders of the Church had already experienced the presence of the glorified Lord at the Lord's Supper. A succession of appearances of the risen Christ to His disciples are connected with the taking of food. He was recognised by the disciples at Emmaus "while He broke bread." The earliest eucharistic prayer that has come down to us (in the *Didache*) cries in Aramaic: "Come, O Lord!" So, too, in the liturgies of the Eastern Church —the Lord appears to the faithful and they receive Him with joy: "Hosanna to the Son of David! Blessed be He that cometh in the name of the Lord!"[74] "To-day the invisible heavenly powers serve with us, for lo! the King of Glory enters; behold the mysterious sacrifice; it is accomplished and is carried in in pomp."[75] "Let all mankind keep silence and stand in fear and trembling and think upon no earthly thing, for the King of Kings, the Lord of Lords cometh to be sacrificed and to offer Himself for the nourishment of them that believe." [76]

It is the sphere of exalted reality into which the faithful are admitted, between fear and joy. Thrilled and trembling with awe the invisible hosts of heaven stand round the altar upon which the sacrifice of Golgotha is re-enacted.[77] This is, however, not only the suffering, but—to emphasise this once more—at the same time the glorified, the living Lord. Therefore to receive His body and blood is to receive eternal life; thus say Irenæus and the early Fathers, this is the spirit of the prayers and praises of the liturgy. And here, again, we are not dealing with an outward, mechanically assumed life; it must be a life morally fruitful, and only in a spirit of moral purity and holiness may the Sacrament be approached. "The Holy to the holy ones!" This warning is pronounced by the priest before the Communion, and the congregation answers, trembling: "One only is holy, one only is Lord, Jesus Christ in the glory of God the Father." Hence this fervent appeal, this continuous, unceasing prayer from the congregation, this ardent wrestling with God, this humble appeal of the unworthy sinner for meekness and cleansing of the heart, which flows like a mighty stream through the whole liturgy. Only thus, only to the contrite, only to him who in his inmost heart prostrates himself before God's grace and mercy, only to him who in spirit bends the knee in fear and trembling before the holiness of the Sacrament, only to him who trusts in God's mercy, only to him who knocks and seeks and prays, and who, realising his own unworthiness, yet throws himself penitent, trembling but hopeful, upon God's grace ; only to such as say, not only with the lips but from the depths of the heart : " I believe, Lord, and I acknowledge Thee to be the Son of God, who came into the world to save sinners, of whom I am the most sinful " [78]—only to such as attain this spiritual state does the sacrament bring blessing, redemption of soul and body, " deliverance from the burden of many sins," " entry into Thy kingdom," [79] eternal life.[80] This effect of the sacrament — physical as well as spiritual, of which the earliest Fathers, beginning with Ignatius, Tertullian, and Irenæus, speak, as well as the earliest liturgical prayers that have come down to us (third century) is frequently reflected in the Communion prayers of the Eastern Church. I will quote one, that of Simeon Metaphrastes of the tenth century (the third of the thanksgiving prayers following the Communion) : " Thou who hast willingly given Thy flesh for my nourishment, Thou fire that consumest the unworthy, consume me not. O my Creator ! Rather penetrate my limbs, my bones, my inmost being, my heart ! Burn up the thorns of my misdeeds ; cleanse my soul and sanctify my spirit and strengthen my joints and bones. Nail me wholly to fear of Thee ! Protect me always, shield and guard me from all deeds or words that destroy the soul. Cleanse, wash, and adorn me, make me better, and teach and enlighten me, that, having become, as a partaker of Thy sacrament, Thy dwelling, all sin and passion may flee from me like fire. . . ." [81] And in another prayer : " O awful mystery, O mercy of God! How can I, even I—unclean that I am, receive the sacred body and blood and become incorruptible!"[82] But it is not only for the individual that the sacrament of the Lord's Supper has a central, living, mystic meaning, but for the whole community, the whole Church, yes, for all mankind. For here the divine mingles with the human, the terrestrial; here in the Eucharist praise and sacrifice are offered to the Lord for the whole world and by the whole world ("Offering Thine to Thee from Thine, for all men and all things!"), and the whole cosmos is hereby potentially ennobled and sanctified in that earthly elements of wine and bread become the glorified body and blood of the Son of God. That is why the idea of all creation assembled in spirit round the eucharistic altar so constantly recurs in the old liturgies of the East. For through Him, through His death, and through the glorification of His risen body, here mystically represented, creation partakes of the glory of the redemption. "Verily heaven and earth are filled with Thy glory through the coming of our Lord and God and Saviour, Jesus Christ," says the old Egyptian liturgy of St Mark.[83] Not only the presence, but also the power of the living Lord is here experienced, and also the approach of the all-embracing kingdom of His glory.[84]

And so in the Lord's Supper we have a particularly powerful expression of the fundamental, all-pervading idea of the great totality, the mystic communion (*ssobornostj*), of the all-embracing, mystical body of Christ.

We find a similar conception in Roman Catholicism. Perhaps some differences appear between the two sister confessions concerning the fundamental idea—nay, rather, experience—of the great mystic communion. We point out this in no spirit of controversy, but merely with a view to defining the characteristics of the Eastern Church. The Eastern Church concentrates her aim not only upon God and the individual soul, as is the case in some of the Protestant sects. For her, too, this individual soul and its relationship to God constitute the most precious, the essential sacredness of religion. But this communion of the soul with God is not a dialogue, but a mighty harmony of many tones, a great organism, a powerful kingdom, a comprehensive brotherhood, a Church of God into which the individual is caught up as a member of the whole body, and which expands and grows into the infinite until it embraces, not only all mankind but the whole of creation, the whole cosmos, in a kingdom of eternal life. It is a cosmic, an œcumenical conception.

I cannot refrain from quoting here the wonderful words of perhaps the greatest Russian theologian (not a professional theologian!) and "church philosopher," Alexei Chomiakov (from his little tract on the Church): "We know that when one of us falls he falls alone, but no man is saved alone. He who is saved is saved within the Church, as a member of the Church, in union with the other members. Does he believe ?—then he is in the communion of faith. Does he love ?—then he is in the communion of love. Does he pray ?—then he is in the communion of prayer. . . . Do not ask : 'What

59

prayer can I spare for the living or the dead, since my prayer does not suffice for myself ? ' For if you do not understand how to pray, of what avail is prayer for yourself ? But it is the Spirit of Love who prays also within you. . . . Nor say : ' Why should another need my prayer, when he prays himself and Christ Himself intercedes for him ? ' When you pray, the Spirit of Love prays within you. Nor say : ' God's judgment is irrevocable '—for your prayers lie in God's path and He has foreseen them. If you are a member of the Church, your prayers are required for all the members of the Church. For if the hand were to say that it had no need of the blood nor of the rest of the body and that it would not give its blood to the rest of the body, the hand would wither. In the same way you are necessary to the Church so long as you are of the Church ; but if you renounce the brotherhood of the Church you will die and cease to be a member. The blood of the Church is prayer one for the other and her breath is praise of the Lord." [85]

The great unity of the Church is not, however, regarded as something formally authoritative, something capable of expression in juridical formulæ. The Eastern Church recognises no formal, juridical authority. For her, Christ, the apostles, the Church councils are not " authority." There is no question here of authority, but of an infinite stream of the life of grace, which has its source in Christ and with which each individual is borne along as a drop or as a ripple.[86] It is with no external, authoritative power that we have to deal, but with the essential principle of life, which permeates each of us, raising us above our petty, individual selves, the life of grace—so long as we have not cut ourselves off from the whole. And the Eastern Church believes that this mighty stream of grace shall sweep along with it and absorb all things, all brethren, all mankind, all creatures that long for deliverance from the bonds of corruption and death, for the " glorious freedom of the children of God."

And this explains, as we have seen, that strong eschatological bias, that yearning, fervent cry of the Church, that joyous expectation of the coming consummation : " Arise, O God, for Thou shalt inherit all nations ! " " Arise, O God, judge the earth, for Thou reignest in eternity ! "

Nor is this mere expectation, mere eschatology ; it is joyful consciousness of the possession now, already, of eternal life : " Christ *is* risen ! " " Truly He is risen ! " [87] " From death to life and from the earth to heaven Christ hath led us, who sing our song of triumph ! " This song of triumph, this jubilant, Easter joy, transfiguring all things, even in the midst of suffering and persecution (as in Soviet Russia at the present time), this cheerful challenge of the power of death and hell, of the merciless and rigid laws of the cosmos, which are now broken and conquered by the superior force of life, this essentially early Christian spirit of faith in the risen Lord—this is, to repeat it once more, the essential life principle, the supreme spirit, the inmost soul of the Eastern Church.

II

TRANSFIGURATION OF THE WORLD AND OF LIFE IN MYSTICISM

CHAPTER I

Joy in Mysticism

THE soul which, after much striving and seeking, has touched the abundant fulness, is flooded with joy; so the mystics tell us. "Joy, joy, joy, tears of joy!" ("*Joie, joie, joie, pleurs de joie!*") cries Pascal at the moment of his decisive mystic experience. The soul feels itself possessed of immeasurable riches, it trembles with silent sighing or is swept away by "inward" jubilant "singing."[88] For all that it deemed of worth hitherto is as nothing beside what it now experiences and knows,[89] what now permeates it and dominates it with incomparable majesty, with overwhelming might and beauty. "O beauty that exceedest all beauty"—"*O hermosura, que excedeis a todas las hermosuras!*"[90] "*O pulchritudo tam antiqua et tam nova!*"[91] The soul has touched the "wells of living water," has drunk eagerly of them,[92] and received a new, eternal life.

All the preaching of primitive Christianity palpitates with the joy of this realisation and possession, exhales this joy, *is* this joy. "The friend of the bridegroom rejoiceth greatly because

63

of the bridegroom's voice : this My joy therefore is fulfilled " [93]—these words are applicable to the whole of primitive Christianity. Eternal life has entered into the world, " and we have seen it, and bear witness and shew unto you that eternal life which was in the Father and was manifested unto us. . . ." " And of His fulness have all we received and grace for grace." [94] This is that costly pearl of which it is said that the merchant who found it sold all to possess it ; this is that treasure in the field of which it is said that the man who found it sold all his possessions and bought that field.[95] Paul speaks of the " unsearchable riches of Christ " ($\grave{a}\nu\epsilon\xi\iota\chi\nu\acute{\iota}a\sigma\tau\sigma\varsigma$ $\pi\lambda\sigma\hat{v}\tau\sigma\varsigma$ $\tau\sigma\hat{v}$ $X\rho\iota\sigma\tau\sigma\hat{v}$),[96] of the " riches of the glory of this mystery which is Christ in you," [97] of the " treasure " which men carry about in " earthen vessels." [98] And in this consciousness the whole inward life of the Christians becomes a joyful song of thanksgiving : " Be filled with the Spirit," cries Paul, " . . . singing and making melody in your heart to the Lord : giving thanks always for all things unto God and the Father in the name of our Lord Jesus Christ." [99] Like a constantly reiterated, unceasing, triumphant *leitmotif* it rings through his letters : " Rejoice evermore. Pray without ceasing. In everything give thanks." " As sorrowful yet always rejoicing." " I am filled with comfort, I am exceeding joyful in all our tribulation." ($\pi\epsilon\pi\lambda\acute{\eta}\rho\omega\mu\alpha\iota$ $\tau\hat{\eta}$ $\pi\alpha\rho\alpha\kappa\lambda\acute{\eta}\sigma\epsilon\iota$, $\acute{v}\pi\epsilon\rho\pi\epsilon\rho\iota\sigma\sigma\epsilon\acute{v}\sigma\mu\alpha\iota$ $\tau\hat{\eta}$ $\chi\alpha\rho\hat{a}$ $\acute{\epsilon}\pi\grave{\iota}$ $\pi\acute{a}\sigma\eta$ $\tau\eta$ $\theta\lambda\acute{\iota}\psi\epsilon\iota$ $\acute{\eta}\mu\hat{\omega}\nu$).[100] Not for nothing are Christians called " children of joy " (in the letter of Barnabas).[101] Filled with this joy they walk boldly to meet death, confessors and martyrs of

Christianity.[102] So are fulfilled the words of Jesus : "These things have I spoken unto you that My joy might remain in you and that your joy might be full." [103]

As a living realisation of this spirit of primitive Christianity, as a living commentary to it, appear also the experiences of the great Christian mystics of later times. Concerning the early Christian recluses and ascetics of the Egyptian desert, we are told by an eye-witness of their manner of life— Bishop Palladius (end of the fourth century) : " They rejoiced, as could be seen, in their life in the desert. Such gladness and rejoicing in the body as theirs is not to be witnessed anywhere on earth. Not one among them was troubled or downcast. . . ." [104] Isaac the Syrian speaks of "waves of inward joy" [105]; from joy spring the outpourings of prayer of Simeon, the New Theologian ; another mystic of the Christian East, Abba Philemon, teaches from the fulness of his spiritual experience : " By constant prayer the eyes of the soul are opened, and it is filled with a great joy and an inexpressible ardour of feeling, and the whole man is spiritualised." [106]

And in the Christian West of the Middle Ages ! Here this spirit is evident in even greater exuberance. For example, Francis of Assisi, after the decisive break with his whole former life, can no longer contain his inward exaltation—it presses outwards,[107] he is as though " drunk in spirit." He shouts and sings.[109] And we read further (in the Italian text of the noble old " Legenda di tre compagni ") of the " unbounded joy and delight in the Holy Spirit " experienced by him and by his disciples—" *smisurata letitia et alegrezza dello Spirito santo."* "*Tanta era la letitia in loro, quasi havessero trovato un gran tesoro nel' evangelico campo della madonna povertà."* [109] They have found an endless treasure in the field of humility ! The Franciscan Jacopone da Todi, poet and mystic, cannot repress his joy—his soul shouts and he feels himself compelled to sing, to declaim, even simply to shout out from excess of feeling.[110] German mediæval mysticism also knows a similar special state of grace, "*genade jubilus.*" [111] And Jacob Boehme felt the very divinity, the inward life in the depths of the divinity, as joy, as a joyful in- and out-pouring of living fulness ; the man who is illumined by the Spirit can already taste thereof. " From the Son, who is the heart of the Father," writes Boehme, " rises the eternal heavenly joy, that eye hath not seen, nor ear heard, nor hath ever risen in the heart of man, as St Paul says. But when a man here on earth is illumined by the Holy Spirit from the spring of Jesus Christ . . ., there enters into his heart and into all his veins such joy that the whole body trembles and the animal spirit triumphs, as though it were in the Holy Trinity, which they alone understand who have been its guests." [112]

Two more examples which are chronologically nearer to us. Our contemporary, Sâdhu Sundar Singh, a Christian mystic of India, speaks in a way similar to Paul's of the abundance of comfort and joy in the midst of tribulation. " I know not why, but my heart was so filled with joy that I could do nothing but sing and preach." [113] And, in con-clusion, the confessions of an anonymous Russian pilgrim of the middle of the nineteenth century, who in the course of his wanderings traversed the whole of European Russia and Siberia (on the way to the Holy Land) ; a man of great capacity for intense inward prayer. (The notes were written on a manuscript in the possession of an old monk of Athos, which was printed in Kasan in 1883.) This pilgrim is possessed by the sweetness of inward prayer, and thereby his whole life is transfigured. It is a curious little book of exceptional weight of religious experience, which reveals to our eyes the quite unexpected, indeed, astounding depth of the religious life of the Russian people (and that, moreover, in its lowest strata !). "So I set out again on my lonely path," the pilgrim relates, "and I felt as I did so much lightness of heart, as though a block of stone had been rolled from my shoulders. Prayer brought me ever-increasing joy, so that many times my heart overflowed with a measureless love for Jesus Christ, and from this sweet spring soothing streams poured through all my bones. The memory of Jesus Christ was so stamped upon my mind, . . . that I felt a joy that cannot be expressed. It sometimes happened that for three days and three nights I entered no human habitation, and I felt a thrill as though I were alone on earth, alone, an abandoned sinner, before the face of a merciful and benevolent God." [114]

In non-Christian mysticism also, the expression of deep inward joy is frequently to be met with. It occurs even in Buddhist texts : "We live in great joy, who possess nothing. Joy is our food, as it is with the radiant gods," etc.[115] But—to make this clear from the outset—in Buddhism there can be no question of this spirit glorifying the world ; for Buddhism there is no absolute, supreme divine reality, its goal being the denial and destruction of every form of world and life. And, therefore, for Buddhism the feeling of joy is merely a transient stage of the way. The highest achievement, the loftiest summit of the Buddhist way is a state in which all joy and every emotion of the heart have long been overcome and cast aside, leaving nothing but emotionless, joyless, frozen "emptiness" of the spirit. "He recognises neither joy nor sorrow," the Sutta-Nipata says of the man of perfect wisdom, "he has no attachments ; therefore he never rejoices." [116]

There is also evidence of inward joy of the soul in the mysticism of the Upanishads. The faces of those who have seen the Atman shine, as in Buddhism the faces of those who have attained the light [117] : "They experience supreme, indescribable blessedness, as they say : ' This is that ' (*i.e.*, as they identify themselves with the Atman).[118] At times even the very Absolute is felt as abundance and fulness of joy. Brahman is joy (or rapture)," we read in the Taittiriya Upanishad. "For out of joy these creatures spring. By joy they live after their birth, and into joy they return when they depart hence." [119] For the rest the pantheistic mysticism of the Upanishads and the Vedânta (and of the corresponding parts of the Mahabhâratâm) is in general decisively influenced by the ideal of an emotionless and rigid indifferentism. In the depths of the infinite and, at the same time, impersonal and indifferent Absolute, all individual feeling, nay, more, all consciousness and perception, are submerged.

Richer in positive tones—tones of the joy and rapture of love—is the Hindu Bhakti mysticism. " Thinking of me and surrendering their life to me . . . they find in me their peace and joy," so speaks Krishna, the highest Being in the Bhagavadgita [120] (for the rest, here, too, cooler tones penetrate from time to time, tones of absolute indifferentism).[121]

A fiery breath of jubilant abandonment and rapture permeates the outpourings of the Tamil saint and poet, Mânikka - Vâśâgar (A.D. 7th-8th centuries). " O thou, our great possession," he prays to Siva, " thou hast held as a sacred shrine my empty, worthless mind, thou hast given me rapturous joy that knows no bounds. . . ." [122] And Kabir, the great Indian mystic, describes his transcendent experience as follows : " Joy for ever, no sorrow, no struggle ! There have I seen joy, filled to the brim, perfection of joy." [123]

CHAPTER II

EXAMPLES OF THE TRANSFIGURATION OF THE WORLD AS EXPERIENCED BY MYSTICS

WHEN the soul is lifted by this joy, in the consciousness that the infinite is present in closest proximity ; nay, more, that it has grasped the infinite, it sees everything with new eyes, it feels within itself and all around a new standard of life : " Old things are passed away ; behold all things are become new ! " (τὰ αρχαῖα παρῆλθεν, ἰδοὺ γέγονε καινά).[124]

> " . . . cuando salia,
> Per toda aquesta vega
> Yam cosa non sabia
> Y el ganado perdì que antes seguia."

" When I came out, I knew nothing any more in the whole extent of this meadow, and I had lost the flocks which I used to tend," says the soul in the mystical poem of the Spaniard, John of the Cross.[125] This state of mind produces not merely an estrangement from the world, but also a glorification of the world and of life.[126] A new world appeared after the spiritual awakening to the eyes of the great Puritan mystic, George Fox. Passing through the sword of flame, he came " in spirit " into the " Paradise of God. . . . All things were new and all the creation gave another smell unto me than before, beyond what words can utter. . . ." [127]   And the experience of Jacob Boehme was similar; after much wrestling and "severe storms," his spirit forced a way, "not without God's help," through the gates of hell into the very heart of the Deity. "But the triumph that was in my spirit I cannot write or speak, nor can it be compared with anything save with the birth of life in the midst of death, with the resurrection of the dead. In this light my spirit straightway looked through all things and saw God in all created things, even in the herbs and the grass." [128]

Symeon, the New Theologian, also tells of new eyes, of a new power, of perception in the glorified man. . . . "He is made worthy to look upon the revelation of great mysteries . . .; I speak of mysteries because, whereas all can see them clearly, they cannot understand. He who is glorified by the newly-creating spirit receives new eyes and new hearing. . . ." [129]   Sister Adelheid of the Unterlinden Convent in Alsace (thirteenth century), leaving the choir after an ecstasy of prayer, believes that she has entered into a new world; the grass, the trees, and even the structure of the convent appear new to her, as though they had just come into existence.[130]   The Italian mystic, Angela of Foligno, in the thirteenth century passed through an experience as soul-shaking as those of George Fox and Jacob Boehme. She felt herself immersed in inward communion with the Holy Spirit, "and wherever I turned my eyes He said to me, ' Behold, that have I created,' and I felt an inexpressible sweetness." [131]   Another time, "The eyes of my soul were opened for a moment and I saw the fulness of God, in which I saw the whole world . . . the sea also and the abyss and all things, but in all this I could see nothing save the divine power in a manner completely beyond expression. And in measureless astonishment my soul cried out and said: 'Truly this world is full of God!' And I felt the whole world as something small. And I saw that the power of God surpasseth all things and filleth all things." [132]

We find corresponding experiences in the non-Christian mystics also. For example, Kabir cries: "Open the eyes of love and behold Him that pervadeth the whole world! Consider it well, and know that this is your own country! . . . I see with eyes open and smile, and behold His beauty everywhere. I utter His name, and whatever I see, it reminds me of Him; whatever I do, it becomes His worship. . . ." Kabir says: "O Sadhu! God is the breath of all breath." [133] "O Father!" sings Mânikka Vâśâgar, "Worlds upon worlds are filled with Thy presence." [134] And Tukaram (seventeenth century A.D.) turns to God with the ecstatic words: "The whole world proclaimeth to me that in it is no place, small even as a grain of mustard seed, which is not full of Thee!" [135] So also for the Persian mystic, the Sufi and Dervish, Baba Kuchi, the whole world is transfigured by his overpowering experience of God: "I opened my eyes and through the radiance of His countenance around me, in everything that my eye perceived—I saw only God!" [136] Ibna'l Farid (an Arabian Sufi of the thirteenth century) also beholds in all things the radiance of the divine beloved and feels himself " drunk, but not with wine " ; he is " penetrated by joy to the depths of his being." " My heart," he says, " danceth, and the twitching of my limbs is like the hand-clapping of a singer, and my spirit is the musician." [137] Another Sufi, Jelal eddin Rumi, feels how the whole world is flooded with waves of love : " Every moment," he says, " from the right hand and from the left soundeth the voice of love." [138]

CHAPTER III

Antinomy in Christianity: Suffering and its Overcoming

The soul is drenched with joy, the world transfigured by love—these are the tones we hear ringing through Christian, and to some extent also through non-Christian, mysticism. But behind this external similarity of spirit there lies a radically different apprehension of the world and of life. Non-Christian mysticism shows a frequent tendency—*e.g.*, in Kabir and in the Persian Sufis—in its spirit of tumultuous jubilation, to shut its eyes optimistically to the evil prevailing in the world. The world becomes entirely, or at any rate chiefly, an "aspect" of the divine, it becomes pantheistically illumined, affirmed and glorified.[139] The problem of evil, suffering, death and sin is either entirely left out of sight, or its whole vast significance is completely underrated [140] : thus these things are looked upon as necessary having regard to the general development,[141] nay more—want and suffering are actually only illusory, deception and sham : nothing is real save joy, the stream of joy !

The Christian idea is quite otherwise. It has its roots in a deeply felt antithesis. It does not in any way close its eyes to the whole power, the whole bitterness of evil, to the painful reality of suffering

74

and sin. "The whole world lieth in wickedness"; "in the world ye shall have tribulation!" "O wretched man that I am! who shall deliver me from the body of this death?" [142] But in the midst of this pain, so really felt, in this world full of evil, death and imperfection, there is revealed to the Christian consciousness, the Christian mysticism—as indeed we know—infinite value. "The Word was made flesh . . . and we beheld His glory, the glory as of the only begotten of the Father, full of grace and truth. . . ." [143] "Surely He hath borne our griefs." [144] He descended to the deepest depths of our desolation, till there came the heart-rending cry of actual experience: "My God, My God, why hast Thou forsaken Me?" Through Him suffering has been transfigured, sanctified; though not abolished, it has become participation in His suffering and His struggle. And further still: voluntarily to take up His Cross, and to follow Him unflinchingly along the "narrow way of the Cross" is the indispensable and enduring condition of participation in His glorified life. For this we are buried with Him, crucified with Him and suffer with Him. And this nearness to Him—though it be also in suffering—is the greatest gain, the richest treasure, the highest joy. With Him even death is life, life eternal! "I am crucified with Christ: yet not I, but Christ liveth in me." "For, as the sufferings of Christ abound in us, so our consolation also aboundeth by Christ." "I am filled with comfort, I am exceeding joyful in all our tribulation." "Who now rejoice in my sufferings for you, and fill up that which is behind of the afflictions of Christ in my

flesh." [145]   Here we have those floods of joy which
we have seen to be so characteristic of primitive
Christianity, so inseparable from it, which constitute
in a word the inmost being of this Christianity, the
elemental, basic power in which it lives and works,
the " Gospel," the " message of joy " !   For it is a
message of joy.   Through His death victory over
death ;   through His resurrection—eternal life !
This is not a mere mood of boundless joy, a purely
emotional riot of feeling, blurred by sentiment,
sensuous or merely æsthetic, as is so often the case
with the Sufis, Indian poets, or other Pantheists; it
is a faith, a firm conviction, having reference to a
concrete fact.   The seed of immortality is already,
now, sown in the world, in a world still imperfect,
still full of sin and death.   But potentially, in
principle, this sin and death are already overcome.
He in whom this seed is sown possesses already a
" treasure," the treasure of eternal life, " the kingdom of God is within you." [146]   Already are fulfilled
the words : " I am with you alway, even unto the end
of the world." [147]   He is the " vine " and we the
" branches," [148] or in the words of Paul : " Christ in
you, the hope of glory " ; " Christ who is our life " ;
" for to me to live is Christ, and to die is gain." [149]

Eternal life has already appeared in the midst of
the world, in the midst of our lives, and through
communion with Him life and the world have
assumed a new value.   " For none of us liveth to
himself, and no man dieth to himself.   For whether
we live, we live unto the Lord ; and whether we die,
we die unto the Lord : whether we live therefore,
or die, we are the Lord's."—" Therefore we are

buried with Him . . . that like as Christ was raised up from the dead by the glory of the Father, even so we also should walk in newness of life." [150] For "the old is passed—behold all is become new." This is a new perception of the world, a new valuation of life, a new appreciation of ourselves also, even of our physical nature. "Know ye not that your body is the Temple of the Holy Ghost which is in you, which ye have of God, and ye are not your own ? for ye are bought with a price : therefore glorify God in your body. . . ." [151]

And the time will come; the kingdom of corruption, death and sin will end, and then will come the complete revelation of glory, the fulness of eternal life : death will be "swallowed up in victory." [152]

Here we have a unique blending of a certain dualism, a recognition of what is merely the transient power of evil and suffering—in all its painful reality —with the consciousness of the presence of eternal life, with the overwhelming consciousness of victory and of the all-prevailing power of this eternal life, which is now already revealed to us, as the fulness of the divine, in the Son, in the person of Jesus. And therein lies the irrationality, the paradox and at the same time the soul-conquering, unageing power of Christianity. This message of the necessity to suffer with Christ and of the saving power of His suffering is in fact "the stumbling-block and foolishness of the Cross" and at the same time the message of eternal life !

Out of this belief that eternal life has entered the world, that "the Word was made flesh and dwelt among us," [153] and passed through the abyss of

77

death—out of this conviction arises the profound uniqueness of the Christian glorification of the world and of life. It is no flippant or obtuse ignoring of pain, no superficial optimism. Rather is it a joyful conviction conquering pain : " In the world ye shall have tribulation : but be of good cheer ; I have overcome the world." [154]

CHAPTER IV

THE " GOOD TIDINGS " AND THE NATURALISM
OF THE ANCIENTS

IN Christian mysticism, as we have seen, the glorification of the world is the outcome of the specific
peculiarities of Christianity. It is inseparably bound
up with the vital nerve, the vital content of the
primitive Christian teaching. This teaching was
essentially concrete. It did not speak of systems
and ideas, but related actual experiences and had
reference to historical events. It was simple and
unscholarly; indeed its simplicity and enthusiasm
made it sound paradoxical, antipathetic and unacceptable to cultured men and scholars—it was
the message of the extraordinary experiences connected with the person of Jesus. This message was
bereft of any purely philosophical intention; it
undertook no philosophical instruction (not for
nothing does Paul speak of the foolishness of the
preaching $\mu\omega\rho\acute{\iota}\alpha$ $\tau o\hat{\upsilon}$ $\kappa\eta\rho\acute{\upsilon}\gamma\mu\alpha\tau o\varsigma$). And yet it
proved, even in the domain of ideas, decisively and
creatively triumphant over both the naturalism
and the dualism of the ancient philosophy.

" That which was from the beginning, which we
have heard, which we have seen with our eyes,
which we have looked upon, and our hands have
handled, of the Word of life (for the life was mani-

fested, and we have seen it, and bear witness, and shew unto you that eternal life, which was with the Father, and was manifested unto us) "—this, though formulated by John the mystic, is the authentic and fundamental content of the whole preaching of the primitive Church.[155] Eternal life has appeared in the world and has overcome the power of death. The seed of immortality is therefore sown in the world and in matter: " Now is Christ risen from the dead, and become the firstfruits of them that slept. . . . The last enemy that shall be destroyed is death." [156] This constitutes a complete subversion of the ancient philosophy's whole conception of the world. It means the end of the rule of those iron laws of the natural order of the world, those laws which were regarded as eternal and immutable even by Plato, and after him by the Platonists and Neo-Platonists, *i.e.*, the representatives of the ancient idealism.

" Evils can never pass away," Plato states through the mouth of Socrates in the *Theætetus*, " for there must always be something which is antagonistic to good. Having no place among the gods in heaven, of necessity they hover around the mortal nature, and this earthly sphere." [157]

The imperfect and the repulsive, suffering, corruption and death are necessary links, indispensable constituents in the life of the cosmos. Were they to be abolished or annulled, the whole life of the world would be thrown into confusion, would come to a standstill. It would be, not a renewal, a rebirth of the world, but a complete annihilation of its existence—this is a favourite philosophical thesis.

This, for example, is the teaching, on the authority of Heraclitus and Pythagoras, of the Idealist Numenius, a forerunner of Neo-Platonism.[158] Plotinus also puts forward with emphasis the same ideas.[159] For the world — as Plato explains in the *Timæus*—is a result of the mixture of mind with necessity, *i.e.*, matter, the embodiment of inertia and irrationality, the source of imperfection and error.[160] In Plotinus matter is actually identified with evil, the original evil ($\pi\rho\hat{\omega}\tau\text{o}\nu$ $\kappa\alpha\kappa\acute{\text{o}}\nu$).[161] Plato and his disciples may call it $\mu\grave{\eta}$ $\breve{\text{o}}\nu$, the "not being," but this "not being" makes itself felt very effectively in the world and in life ; it sets its seal upon the whole life of the cosmos, the seal of transience, ugliness and suffering,[162] and like a painful harping strain this idea pervades the whole development of the philosophy of Plato and the Platonic school, in harsh and constant dissonance with the praise, so enthusiastic and indeed so abundant, of the beauty, perfection and harmony of the universe that is to be found in the writings of these very philosophers—*i.e.*, Plato, Plotinus, and their disciples.[163] Hence the doctrine of escape from the world, turning aside from the world, " of the flight of the solitary to the solitary " ($\phi\upsilon\gamma\grave{\eta}$ $\tau\text{o}\hat{\upsilon}$ $\mu\acute{\text{o}}\nu\text{o}\upsilon$ $\pi\rho\grave{\text{o}}\varsigma$ $\tau\grave{\text{o}}\nu$ $\mu\acute{\text{o}}\nu\text{o}\nu$)[164] ; the body as the tomb or prison of the spirit,[165] the life of the philosopher as a constant preparation for death ($\mu\varepsilon\lambda\acute{\varepsilon}\tau\eta$ $\tau\text{o}\grave{\upsilon}$ $\theta\alpha\nu\acute{\alpha}\tau\text{o}\upsilon$),[166] anticipation of death as a deliverance ; the world a vast, joyless gulf, a prison, a place of lies and spiritual ruin.[167] And no prospect of a fundamental change ! The individual soul may indeed escape, but the world as a whole dwells in evil, and for it there is no escape. For evil and suffering are, as we have seen, necessary consequences of its constitution, immutable conditions of the general beauty and harmony of the cosmos. Were there in the world no worse beside the better, there could be no Providence; the intelligence which rules the world does not even desire that all things in the world should be good : this would prejudice the general purpose of this completed work of art.[168] The beauty of the cosmos lies precisely in the fact that each of its limbs should be in its place : " if, therefore, hideous groans resound in the darkness of Tartarus, in their proper place even these groans are beautiful." " Therefore evil vanisheth not from the world." Such is the teaching of Plotinus, the great idealist and mystic.[169]

In the world prevail the artistically perfect, but entirely rigid, soulless and pitiless laws of nature, the cycle of life and death, the eternal up and down. No end, no finality is to be seen in this stream of growth and decay, this sinister fever of an illusory existence, this realm of corruption and death—otherwise known as world harmony—where every single individual thing is destroyed for the sake of the life of the whole [170]; for this life of the whole is merely a sum, an " equivalent " of an infinite succession of deaths.[171] So it is, and remains, unchangeable. " Ever the same, from the beginning to the end is the cycle ($\pi\epsilon\rho\acute{\iota}o\delta o\varsigma$) of mortal things," says the Platonist Celsus. " And it is a law of fate that by means of firmly-fixed cycles the same thing should happen in the past, the present and the future." [172] No really progressive development towards an end, no hope of a final victory of life! The world of incorruptible and eternal ideas, to which alone, according to the teaching of Plato, the true and full reality belongs, capitulates before the unyielding power of the " not being," *i.e.*, matter ; the power of the ideal, divine actuality breaks itself against the natural, changelessly defiant *status quo* of the cosmic process.[173]

And then there is the Stoical philosophy, with its glorification and deification of these same laws of nature! This we have already in part in Platonism, but the Stoics lack that painful contradiction, that teaching of another, truer being, that exhortation to escape from the world. For the Stoics the empirical being is also the norm ; there is no other, higher reality. Evil, imperfection, suffering and ruin of the individual constituents are therefore finally compensated and justified by the serenely untroubled, triumphantly overriding life of the whole.[174] What inspired, abundant praise is offered to that beauty, that majestic harmony of the cosmos![175] But one has only to open the *Meditations* of the most deeply feeling of the Stoics, the solitary imperial thinker, Marcus Aurelius. There we find, side by side with such hymns of praise to the cosmos, a profound lassitude, a melancholy, hopeless resignation, apparent in his contemplation of this all-engulfing, ceaselessly roaring maelstrom of the cosmic life.[176] And once, even, the piteous cry escapes him : "How long then ? " (μέχρι τίνος οὖν).[177]

Christianity proclaims—in the paradoxical and, to the worldly-wise, unacceptable message of the

Cross and Resurrection—the suppression of the cosmic laws, their coming, final suppression! Together with the whole creation we groan and travail, waiting for "the adoption, the redemption of our body" (τὴν ἀπολύτρωσιν τοῦ σώματος ἡμῶν). "Because the creature itself also shall be delivered from the bondage of corruption (ἀπὸ τῆς δουλείας τῆς φθορᾶς) into the glorious liberty of the children of God." "That God may be all in all." "And He that sat upon the throne said, Behold I make all things new!" [178]

Similar expectations of a complete renewal of the world are to be found already in late Judaism. In the concluding chapters of the Book of Isaiah we read: ". . . For, behold, I create new heavens and a new earth: and the former shall not be remembered, nor come into mind." . . . "For as the new heavens and the new earth, which I will make, shall remain before me, saith the Lord, so shall your seed and your name remain." [179] In the (Ethiopian) Book of Enoch is written: "The first heaven shall vanish and die away and a new heaven shall appear and thereafter shall there be countless weeks unto eternity in goodness and righteousness, and sin shall never more be spoken of unto eternity." [180] And the expectation of a coming resurrection of the dead and of an "eternal life" is frequently to be met with in the religious literature of late Judaism (beginning with the Book of Daniel) [181] in which the influence of the Parsee eschatology is possible, indeed extremely probable.

But in Christianity it was not merely, as was the case with Judaism, hope of a distant and as yet nebulous future, but, first and foremost, the preaching of something already experienced as a definite and concrete event : salvation has appeared, the victory over death is already won—in the resurrection of the Lord ! The faith of primitive Christianity did not therefore depend upon mere expectations, but upon what had already appeared as an accomplished fact. Anyone who loses sight of this important religious distinction is shutting his eyes to the understanding of Christianity and its origin. Herein lies indeed the specific and fundamental, the indispensable, organic peculiarity of the Christian religious experience and of the Christian preaching ; this is also what gave to the preaching of the primitive Church that spirit of joy and jubilation, that contagious, impelling force (" This is the victory that overcometh the world, even our faith ! "). This made it in reality the " message of joy." [181a]

For now, already, we may say " thanks be to God, which giveth us the victory ($\tau\hat{\omega}$ $\delta\iota\delta\acute{o}\nu\tau\iota$ $\dot{\eta}\mu\hat{\iota}\nu$ $\tau\grave{o}$ $\nu\hat{\iota}\kappa o\varsigma$) through our Lord Jesus Christ." [182] Eternal life *has* entered the world, Christ is risen, the first-fruits of the dead ! This message contained a seed of infinite potentiality, the seed of a complete revolution in the apprehension of the world and of life.

CHAPTER V

TWO CURRENTS IN THE HISTORY OF CHRISTIAN CONSCIOUSNESS IN THE MIDDLE AGES: GLOOMY DUALISM AND THE TRANSFIGURATION OF THE WORLD THROUGH RELIGION

I

TWO currents therefore can be traced through the whole history of Christianity in its relationship to the world : a dualism, relative indeed, and in principle superseded, and a joyful transfiguration of life and of the world. These two tendencies at times attain to a harmonious and organic balance (especially in mysticism) and this rich and fruitful co-operation produces the Christian philosophy and the Christian life in all fulness, but sometimes the balance is lost ; they become mutually antagonistic, or ignore each other, and then they give rise to religious decadence or aberration.

In the past history of Christianity the extreme dualistic tendency frequently stood out with special prominence. This, moreover, was quite natural, for a definite ethical dualism is in general an indispensable and vital constituent of the Christian consciousness, just as is the painful and acute perception of the present, though transitory, " wicked " state of life and of the world. But in reality— as appears with special frequency during the Middle

Ages—this ethical dualism becomes almost a metaphysical dualism (although a radically metaphysical dualism is not officially recognised by the dogma of the Church). The whole complex of the world and life seemed to the darkened, frightened imagination a realm of the devil, a playground of demoniacal powers. Not seldom it extinguishes the overwhelming and uplifting perception of the already granted presence and nearness of eternal life, this perception that was so characteristic of early Christianity, in spite of all its eschatological expectations of the coming judgment and consummation. In the Middle Ages therefore religion is often apprehended as something wholly transcendent while leaving a shadow of darkness upon the world and life.

But of special importance for us, in contrast to this gloom which from time to time has gained the upper hand in the history of the Christian consciousness, are the true examples of the fulness of the Christian spirit. I mean those saints and spiritual heroes in whom shone forth with special power the fire and light of love, of that all-embracing love which flows out upon all creatures and glorifies them.

Let us linger a brief moment with the old Fathers of the Desert of the Christian East. In some of these stern, hard ascetics, who fled from the world into the wilderness, there would burst forth suddenly an ardent, one might almost say an uncontainable love, a boundless sympathy towards every creature. From this arose a feeling of solidarity, of brotherhood extending even to unreasoning creation. Isaac the Syrian has described this state. He throws out the question: τί ἐστιν καρδια ἐλεήμων; ("What is a compassionate heart?") and answers: it is "a kindling of the heart over every creature (καῦσις καρδίας ὑπὲρ πάσης τῆς κτίσεως)—over mankind, the birds, animals, demons and the whole creation. And when he remembers them or contemplates them, the tears well from his eyes out of the great pity which grips his heart. And his heart feels itself moved and possessed, and cannot bear to see or hear any creature suffer hurt, or the slightest pain." [183] The stories of some of the Fathers of the Nitrian and Syrian deserts may serve as a living commentary on these words. For instance, a contemporary relates of a certain Abbas Theo (fourth century) that " he went forth from his cell by night and gave drink to the wild beasts which would gather round him." [184] Another venerable man " had reached such a high state of spiritual perfection that he would (fearlessly) meet a lion which came into his cave and feed it from his lap." [185] There is a touching old story of the friendship between a holy hermit and a she-wolf which would visit him regularly at his meal-times and share his bread. [186] On the other hand, the wild animals appearing in these stories are in their turn morally ennobled by their inter-course with the saintly men and lose their wild-ness and cruelty. [187] Paul the Hermit once said: " Whoever hath attained purity findeth all things subject unto him, like Adam in Paradise before the fall." [188] The harsh and savage in nature is here glorified through the power of Christian love and perfection as was also later the case with Francis of

Assisi and some of the Russian saints (*e.g.*, Sergius of Radonesch). This is indeed the "power of Christ: to His honour the unreasoning understand; to His honour the wild become tame" says Sulpicius Severus in his account of the Eastern anchorites.[189]

By so much the more is the beauty of the world transfigured for the enlightened eye, that beauty which so frequently leads into temptation, and which on that account is so often shunned by the ascetics. An example of this enlightened state is described by John Climax (sixth century), one of the sternest teachers of the ascetic life : "When a man," he says, "saw a woman of unusual beauty, he praised the Creator for her. The sight of her kindled within him the love of God, and a flood of tears streamed from his eyes. And it was wonderful to see how that which would have proved the undoing of another became for him in supernatural manner the crown of victory. If such a man in such cases always feels and conducts himself in this way, he has become a partaker of incorruptibility even now, before the general resurrection." [190] Similarly, the hermit Antony the Great says to a philosopher who sought him out in the desert : "My book is the whole visible creation, and it lies open before me whenever I wish to read in it the words of God." [191]

II

It is particularly instructive to linger over the religious outlook of the mediæval West. For the contrast between a gloomy dualism, which entirely rejects the world, and a mystical transfiguration of the world and life through the power of love here reveals itself with special weight and plasticity. And, moreover, the psychological material is presented in particular fulness and variety.

The devil! Everywhere the devil! He is felt and sensed at every step, in every circumstance of life, in the whole of surrounding nature—that is the key-note of what may be called the dualistic spirit of the Middle Ages. The beauty of the world is temptation, a snare laid by the devil to catch souls. There was, for instance, a cleric who possessed a voice so beautiful that to listen to him was rapture—but this was the devil who had entered into the body of a dead cleric. When he was driven out by exorcism the body fell to pieces and stank (*exivit, cadavere mox corruente ac fœtente*).[192] The cuckoo calling in the monastery garden is a device of the devil's cunning.[193] Even the temple of God, even divine service provide no security from the countless hosts of demons that circle round us. To many monks it was given to see them creeping about in the church in the form of toads, cats, dogs, apes or swine, or of innumerable little black men with fiery faces.[194] Or Satan would appear suddenly in the form of a flying dragon or of a gigantic, fiercely gleaming, lurid eye.[195] The demons hover in the air, they bear down upon us in serried ranks, they fill the whole atmosphere—numberless, endless! [196] They pester the celebrants and the monks singing in the choir and throw them into confusion; they cause them to make mistakes in the singing and in the performance of the ritual; they compel the monks to cough, sneeze and spit and thus lead the surrounding congregation into temptation.[197] Even the consummation of the Holy Sacrament does not drive the demons out of the church.[198] And outside the consecrated walls it is worse still. Particularly terrifying are the nightly apparitions of demons, the nightmares and terrors with which they persecute the monks in their dormitories where they swarm round the beds of the sleepers.[199] And often out of the darkness will suddenly rise the form of a loathsome monster or a black giant.[200]

If this is the state of affairs within the precincts of the monastery, within the church walls, what must it be in the world outside? The devil is not infrequently regarded as the overlord dwelling in visible nature. The holy penitents and men of God in building their cells, their monasteries and churches, had often to wrest the land in battle, so to speak, from the clutches of demons.[201] The sinister and gigantic in nature, such as strangely shaped masses of rock, are declared to be the work of the devil; and even outstanding creations of human art, which excite the imagination, are also frequently traced to this same mysterious demonic origin. The life of the outside world, too, is set constantly with the snares of the devil, but already here he often works more ruthlessly and openly than within the monastery walls. In the mediæval collections of didactic stories there are many examples of the devil's interference in the lives of men, amounting even to acts of violence.[202]

This not infrequently gave rise to an oppressive, terrifying feeling of enslavement, a fearful spiritual obsession. " I am often seized with a sudden terror," says the novice in the *Dialogus Miraculorum* of Cæsarius von Heisterbach, " and that even in the choir as well as in other places. What is the cause of this shuddering (*hujus horripilationis*) ? " And the older, more experienced monk answers : " It comes from the presence of the demons (*ex præsentia dæmonum est*)." [203] This obsession of the spirit is revealed with particular force in the *Revelations of the Abbot Richalmus concerning the Craft and Cunning of the Demons* (late thirteenth century), in its way a classic. Here terror of demons becomes an actual, indescribable frenzy, a real mania, reaching a point of grotesque absurdity which borders upon dementia.[204] " As a man sunken in the sea is surrounded by water—above, below, and on all sides, so the demons beleaguer men (*sic et dæmones homini undique circumfunduntur*)." [205] " They are ever, ever with us ! " [206] " They are like a mist, enshrouding men on all sides " [207]; " countless are they, like the grains of dust which dance in the sunbeams ; they surround man like a dense, impenetrable wall (*circumvallant hominem*)." [208] " The whole world is full of them ! The whole air is nothing but a dense mass of demons (*quædam spissitudo eorum*)." [209]

And there are many other things besides this fear of demons to darken the religious outlook of mediæval Christianity : the consciousness of the transitoriness, the fragility of all earthly things and especially of the illusoriness and corruptibility of earthly beauty and the beauty of the body. The Middle Ages are indeed, as we know, full of violent pictures of death and its dominion.[210]

III

But, as we have already indicated to some extent, this fear and anxiety, this horror, this gloomy disavowal of the world, do not speak the only, or the last word in the religious life of the Middle Ages. Even in the Middle Ages there is not infrequently a consciousness of the presence of the divine, even here on earth among earthly surroundings. This communion with the heavenly world is especially perceptible during divine service, or in any of the places more or less sanctified by prayer and penitence: in church or within the monastery precincts, "*Ubique credimus divinam esse præsentiam,*" so we read in the old monastic rule of St Benedict, "*. . . maxime tamen hoc sine aliqua dubitatione credamus, cum ad opus divinum adsistimus.*" [211] The monastery chronicles or collections of pious legends, for instance, tell us of many appearances of these heavenly powers descending to commune with man. Many of these narratives are full of profound religious pathos and mystic fervour. Thus it was granted to some pious monks, during a service at night, to see the Mother of God, with the Child in her arms, pass through the rows of brothers singing in the choir and stand still in front of those who were fervent and vigilant in prayer, hold out the divine Child towards them and bless them [212] or give them from a chalice a wondrous draft of inexpressible sweetness (which drink, the pious narrator declares, " signifies the grace of devotion—*gratia devotionis*—for by its power the singers are strengthened, by its sweetness the weariness of the vigil is changed to joy ").[213] Or they would see, as though keeping faithful watch, the Saviour or His Blessed Mother walk through the dormitory by night and bless the sleepers.[214] Even death is rich in grace within these consecrated monastery walls during these night hours which are glorified by the descent of the heavenly powers.[215]

The most blessed experience, however, is to be present, or to take part in the consummation of the Holy Sacrifice, the Sacrament of Sacraments, which unites the earthly world with the heavenly, as the invisible heavenly hosts fall in awe and trembling upon their knees and join in the service,[216] and the Lord Jesus is at once the slain Sacrifice and the High Priest who, invisible to mortal eye, stands in the midst, consummates the great mystery, and blesses the worshippers.[217] And how often have the penitent men and women, filled with the fire of love, not only felt the nearness of their crucified Lord, but also actually looked upon Him during the divine service or in hours of solitary prayer—sometimes scourged at the stake, His blood flowing,[218] sometimes bowed beneath the load of the Cross,[219] sometimes stretched in His death agony upon the Cross [220]—sometimes as risen from the dead and pointing to His wounds—His pierced hands and feet.[221]

There arose an atmosphere of intensest consciousness of the nearness of the divine life,[222] which is exhaled from many of these chronicles ; whereas, as we have seen, other mediæval sources palpitate with terror of the power of the devil attacking man from all sides. Sometimes these two states of mind—apparently so sharply opposed—intermingle in the same work.

This perception of the nearness of the divine life

is not confined to the interior of the church or monastery, but flows outside, pervades also the world, and calls into life a succession of legends of fragrant beauty and often of overwhelming religious power. If, for instance, we open the old French collection of the miracles of the Holy Virgin, written by Gautier de Coincy (thirteenth century), one of the most fragrant books of the Middle Ages, or the ancient German collections on the same subject, we are at once enveloped in the pure and intoxicating air of this unsophisticated faith. Yes, this faith did often in reality look upon the world with the pure eyes of an innocent child, and divine wonderful mysteries even in the life of every day. And it transfigured this life, regardless of all its defects, through the sense of something divine and heavenly (and at the same time irresistibly moving and beautiful)—and especially through the feeling of the closeness of a meek [223] and touchingly loving God descending to us in our vale of sorrow and revealing Himself to those who are themselves of humble heart. For, as we have said, the divine is near us, meets us at every step, though we know it not; for in the form of the poor and the beggar, or of that wanderer standing before your door, or of the outcast there upon the road, stands Christ Himself, asking your compassion, your love. "Verily I say unto you: Inasmuch as ye have done it unto one of the least of these My brethren, ye have done it unto Me"—the whole mediæval period is stamped with the deep, overwhelming imprint of these words of Jesus, which have coloured its pious legends and the amazingly joyful experiences of its saints. [224]

The deepest impression, however, of this union of the earthly with the heavenly, this condescension of the heavenly, this glorification and deification of the earthly being was received by the Middle Ages —as we have seen—in the Sacrament of the Lord's Supper. This stands in the very centre of their religious life. Around the Lord's Supper the Middle Ages weave their most splendid religious legends, visions and ecstasies.[225] Everything that comes in contact with that supreme Sacrament of the *daily descent of God*,[226] is either glorified or consumed as unworthy.[227] There is an example of a pious sister falling on her knees in the snow when she heard the distant ringing of the bell that announced the Elevation. And behold! In the middle of the snow, in the depth of winter, green grass immediately sprang up in the place.[228] From this same source — adoration of the Sacrament — that most enthralling and marvellous of stories in the semi-religious, semi-profane literature of the Middle Ages —the story of the Holy Grail [229]—drew its mystical inspiration.

Lastly, the language of nature was not merely dead or terrifying to the religiously minded of the Middle Ages. We have no little evidence of the deep impression made upon sensitive natures by the beauty of their natural surroundings.[230] And not infrequently the pious man learns to rise from the beauty of creation to the beauty of the Creator.[231] Moreover, there is opened, to meet the quick sensitiveness to the beauty of nature, the need shared also by pious souls to take delight in this beauty, a whole domain in which it can have free play, unhampered by the gloomy restrictions of the ascetic philosophy ; I mean those legends, often so fresh and unsophisticated, in which the earthly Paradise makes its appeal to the religious imagination with all the charm of an immaculate, unspoiled nature—legends which are still often pervaded, as are often also stories of the Holy Grail, by a breath of ecstasy.[232]

It cannot therefore be denied that even in the specific atmosphere of mediæval piety, apart from and side by side with its notes of gloom, there was a tendency towards a religious transfiguration of the world and life. These sparks blaze into brilliant flame in the lives of the great mystics, who were possessed by the overwhelming consciousness of the nearness of God. And among these the first is Francis of Assisi.

IV

We have already given a few examples of the transfiguration of the world in the experience of the mediæval mystics.[233]   But it is worth while to linger a little longer over this great spiritual treasure-house which here opens before us.

Francis of Assisi, " wholly sunk in the love of God," in the words of the old story of his life which comes from the circle of his most intimate disciples, " saw in every creature the goodness of God in its perfect form (*in qualibet creatura bonitatem Dei perfecte cernebat*), wherefore he was possessed by an extraordinary love for created things (*propter quod singulari et viscerosa dilectione afficiebatur ad creaturas*), particularly those which as living symbols and images

97   G

reminded him of God." [234] In the old accounts of Francis this fact rises before us like a great poem. They are a song of love, of joyful ecstasy, of reverential pity and loving humility spreading over the whole world, over all creatures, and first and foremost over all that is lowly, humbly beneficent and gentle in nature : the lambs,[235] the turtle-doves,[236] the swallows,[237] the lilies of the valley and the sweet-smelling herbs,[238] " Sister Water," " *la quale è molto utile et humile et pretiosa et casta* " (" which is very useful and humble and precious and modest "), " our mother the earth, which bears us and guides (*governa*) us, and brings forth various fruits, the brightly-coloured flowers and the grass ! " [239] and at the same time his ardent poet's soul is no less filled with the love of everything in creation which is radiantly beautiful and bright and vigorous—of " my brother fire, noble and useful above all created things,[240] by which Thou, O Lord, illuminest the night, and he is beautiful and joyous and vigorous and strong " (*ed ello è bello et iocundo et robusto et forte*),[241]—for " of all unreasoning creatures he loved fire most ardently, because of its beauty and usefulness," says an old biographer [242]—also of " brother wind," " sister moon," and the stars, " which Thou, O Lord, hast created in the heavens, bright, beautiful and precious," the brilliant and mighty " brother sun," who in his splendour and brilliance is an image of the Highest :

> " *Laudato sie, Misignore cum tucte le tue creature,*
> *Spetialemente messor lo frate sole . . .*
> *Et ello è bello e radiante cum grande splendore,*
> *De te Altissimo, porta significatione.*" [243]

For Francis, the whole creation is living and close to his heart. He preaches not only to the birds, but also to the flowers. He summons the rocks and vineyards, the gardens and the springs to join in the general praise of the Lord.[244] He cares for the bees [245] and the swallows [246]; he plays with " sister cicada " and " brother pheasant," [247] nay, more,— he even walks upon the stones with reverence and awe, for love of Him who is named the " corner-stone " (*super petras etiam quum ambularet, cum magno timore et reverentia ambulabat*),[248] and lifts the worm carefully out of his path, lest the foot of the wanderer crush it : " *circa vermiculos etiam nimio flagrabat amore* "—even " the worms kindled within him infinite love," says his bio-grapher.[249] And then there is the ardent love of Francis for mankind, which is revealed in his preaching and missionary work.

Even the imperfect, the crude and the vicious in nature, and sin in man, offer no barrier to the love of Francis, nor do they hide from his eyes the image of God dwelling in man, the reflection of the divine which fills the whole world, makes us all members of one great family—brothers and sisters in God. And this love is at the same time an illuminating and a spiritually bracing power. By it the cruel " brother wolf " is tamed.[250] By this measureless stream of loving humility the brutal and savage robbers are touched and overpowered.[251] By this love many sinful hearts, coming under the influence of Francis, have been carried away along with him and enrolled in the service of Christ. The rough powers of nature are softened as they come into touch with his inward

light, overpowered, even imbued with this same love.
" And there is indeed no cause for wonder," we read
in the recollections of his disciples, " that the fire and
other unreasoning creatures should always obey and
honour him, for we who were with him have ourselves very often seen how he was so filled with love
towards them, how he felt such delight in them and
how his spirit was moved by such compassion and
sympathy for them (*ipse tantum afficiebatur, ad eos et
in eis tantum delectabatur et circa ipsos tanta pietate
et compassione movebatur spiritus eius*), that he could
not bear that they should be despised. And possessed by inward and outward ecstasy, he would
converse with them as though they had understanding, whereby his soul was often filled with rapturous
love of the Lord." [252]

All living creatures approach him with confident
love. The birds listen eagerly to his preaching and
await his blessing.[253] The grasshopper perches on
his hand and at his bidding sings its joyful praise of
the Lord.[254] A river bird hides in his hands and
refuses to fly away.[255] A captured fish, which he sets
free in the water, plays in the water near him and
does not swim away until Francis dismisses it with
his blessing.[256] A wild hare nestles to him, hops into
his lap under the folds of his robe and will not leave
him,[257] and before his death there collected an
" immense flock " of the swallows he had loved so
dearly and had cared for so greatly throughout his
life [258] and, circling round the roof of the house
in which the dying Francis lay, seemed to praise the
Lord with their sweet notes.[259]

Round Francis, as with other great saints, a new

spiritual atmosphere, a new spiritual *milieu* came into being ; the joyous consciousness of an exalted and transfigured reality, of a breath of eternal life. " Therefore," his intimate disciples tell us, " we saw him rejoice, inwardly and outwardly, over almost all creatures, in such measure that when he touched them and contemplated them his spirit seemed to be not upon earth but in heaven (*in tantum videbamus ipsum interius et exterius lætari quasi in omnibus creaturis, quod ipsos tangendo vel videndo non in terra, sed in cælo ejus spiritus videbatur*)." [260] And there poured from the mouth of Francis a joyous song of praise. The whole world is ennobled, all creatures and the whole of life, even the trials and sorrows of life ; for everything gives cause to praise and thank God : " Blessed be Thou, O Lord, in these things which for love of Thee forgive and endure sickness and tribulation." Even death is glorified : " *Laudato si, Misignore, per sora nostra morte corporale !* " (blessed art Thou, O Lord, for our sister—death of the flesh !) [261] For, possessed by the love of Christ —the centre and essence of his whole inward life— Francis has apprehended in Him the world, his brothers, and all creatures (at every step the creatures call Christ to his mind [262]), and the whole of life, and even death, thus experiencing anew what Paul felt when he said—" For to me to live is Christ, and to die is gain." [263]

Echoes of this joy, blessing the world, of this communion of love with the creature, ring out also from the lives of those disciples of Francis who were closest to him in spirit. Birds alight on the hands and arms of John of Parma while he is at prayer.

Of John of Alverna we read : " Once, at night, he was filled with such rapturous light that he saw all creatures in their Creator (*vidit omnia creata in Creatore*), both the earthly and the heavenly." [264] This same mood appears in other monuments of the early Franciscan spirit, such as the allegorical story of the " mystical marriage of Saint Francis with Lady Poverty " (" *Le mistiche nozze del beato Francesso con madonna Povertà* "), so fragrant and so touching in its childlike grace. When Lady Poverty, who has come to live with the brothers, asks them where their monastery is, they show her from the mountain-top the whole world stretched out below them—hills, woods, meadows and rivers : " That is our monastery ! " All this world is inundated by the streams of God's love and beauty, and these streams press upon the soul, penetrate it, " beleaguer " it from all sides : *O amor, divino amore— perchè m'hai assediato ?* (" O love, divine love, why hast Thou so pressed upon me ? "), cries Jacopone da Todi, in trembling confusion.[265]

A deep consciousness of the beauty of God in the world also pervades the pages of a Provençal tract of the fourteenth century : *Scala divini amoris*,[266] which had its source in the same *milieu* and exhales the same spirit as the earlier Franciscanism. " I maintain," we read here, " that in every one of the creatures that are under heaven there is a sweetness, a fragrance, a harmony and a beauty." But in all this—" *dins tota sabor e dins tota suavetat e dins tota odor e dins tot cant e dins tota beutat* "—is " the beauty and sweetness of God present, the nearness of God, yea, God Himself, and withal nearer and more

immediate than any of these things is in itself."
Thus there is in the purity of the air a wonderful
delight; wherefore men love to climb to the summits
of high mountains, and some birds, caught by these
floods of sweetness that pervade the air, remain as
though in ecstasy hovering motionless in one spot—
"*per la suavetat del tocamen de l'aire quels toca al cor,
estan en l'aire eo raubit.*" And fishes "raise themselves out of the water by night and from the sweet
contact of the air and dew they bring forth precious
gems. Great therefore must be the sweetness of the
air's touch which throws the birds into ecstasy and
through which the fishes bring forth jewels!"
And in all elements and in all creatures rings the
refrain of the divine song—*melodia de cant*, and "one
of the greatest wonders of this age it is that my soul
doth not die nor lose itself in madness when it
heareth how heaven and earth are filled with this
song. . . ." God and the world sing together anti-
phonally, as it were: "Therefore God begins His
balada and says, '*Amors!*' and all creation answers:
'Thou hast created us!' And '*mosenher san Johan
Evangelista*' says of this *doussa balada* that he heard
how it was sung by all creatures on earth, in heaven
and in the waters: 'Love, Thou hast created us,
that we may love!' For men this is the fourth
stage of the ascent into the palace of love; when the
soul is so thrilled with the great sweetness of that
music which all creatures bring forth in praise of God
that it neither sees, nor hears, nor feels, for it forgets
itself and remembers only the Lord." In short,
"in all beauty that is in created things," man
should perceive and contemplate—"*la cara res-*

plandent de Ghesu Christ qui resplandis e ri ins la beutat de las creaturas "—" the radiant countenance of Jesus Christ, which shines and smiles in the beauty of created things." [267]

The same picture of Christ in created things, or more accurately of all created things ennobled and illumined in Christ, has also been perceived by a German visionary, Agnes Blannbekin of Vienna (end of the fourteenth century). " She was swept away," we read in her *Revelations*, " into an indescribable light, and in this divine light she saw a Man beautiful above all children of men . . . and in this Man and in this divine light she saw the elements and the creatures and the things which are made from them, both small and great, stand out in such brilliance, that each of them, however small, appeared a hundred times more brilliant than the sun . . . even the smallest grain of corn or pebble. And the light of the present world compared with this brilliance would have seemed dark like the moon when she is covered by a dark cloud. And created things appeared so clearly in this radiance that each could be distinguished by its quality ; a green grain, a red rose, etc. But among all the elements and created things the earth was the most splendid. And this because God took His body from the earth ; . . . and because during the Lord's Passion the earth was drenched with the blood of the Saviour. . . . All this was in this Man, *i.e.*, in Christ." [268]

The transfiguration of creation through the power of the love which embraces all things, all beings in prayer and bears them upwards to their original source, we meet with in the works of one of the greatest German mystics of the Middle Ages, Heinrich Suso. He was asked what his thoughts were when he sang Mass and began the preface: "*sursum corda....*" The words came from his mouth with such extraordinary religious fervour (*als recht begierlich*) that those who heard it were filled with a yearning of the soul. He replied: "When I pronounce the words, '*sursum corda*' during the Mass, it usually happens that my heart and soul are dissolved within me from godlike pain and longing (*von göttlichen Jammer und Begierde*), so that in that hour my heart is transported out of itself"; and he was filled with wonderful visions, "in which," he says, "I was borne up to God and through me all creatures."

"The first vision was thus. I saw with my inward eyes myself in all that I am, body and soul and all my faculties, and placed around me all creatures that God ever created in heaven and earth and in the four elements, each individually with its name, were it bird of the air, beast of the forest, fish of the water, leaf and grass of the earth and the uncountable sands of the sea and all the little grains of dust which dance in the sunshine and all the drops of water which ever fell in dew or snow or rain or will ever fall! And I wished that each one of them might have a sweet soaring song within it distilled from the essence of my heart and that they might raise new, exalted praises to the beloved God from eternity to eternity.

"And joyfully the loving arms of the soul opened and stretched out towards the inexpressible throng of the creatures, and it was my wish to inspire them with eagerness, as a leader of a choir stimulates his fellow-singers, to sing joyfully and to raise their hearts to God : *sursum corda*." [269]

Here, as in Francis's hymns of praise, all creatures are ennobled, all are members of one great family ; nay, more—they are summoned to be members of one great communion, of one Church embracing the whole world and the whole creation, singing praises to her Lord at the moment of the consummation of the eucharistic sacrifice.

The mystical glorification of the world during the Middle Ages perhaps found its highest expression in the experiences of the English mystic of the end of the fourteenth century, Lady Julian of Norwich, in her *Revelations of Divine Love*. The world is small and nothing worth. God showed her in a vision "a little thing, the quantity of a hazel-nut, lying in the palm of my hand ; and, to my understanding, it was round as any ball." And it was said to her : "'It is all that is made.' I marvelled how it might last, for methought it might fall suddenly to nought for littleness." It cannot satisfy the cravings of the soul : "all that is beneath God, suffices not to us." In order to find real satisfaction in God we must free the soul of all that is made : "No soul is rested, till it be noughted of all that is made." And yet God loves this world which, in comparison with Him, is infinitely small and mean: "It lasts and ever shall, for God loves it. And so all-thing hath its being through the love of God."

"In this little thing," *i.e.*, the universe, Julian continues, "I saw three parts : the first is that God made it. The second is that He loves it. The third is that God keeps it." [270] And in this light of

God's love the world assumes for this mystic a new meaning, a new nobility, a new worth. " I saw all-thing that He has made. It is great and fair and large and good. But the cause why it showed so little to my sight was because I saw it in the presence of Him that is its Maker. For to a soul that sees the Maker of all-thing, all that is made seems full little." The great worth and highest merit of the universe lies in this, that it is a fruit of the divine love and also has love as its goal. God " made all-thing that is made for love, and through the same love it is kept and ever shall be without end." For " God is all-thing that is good, and the goodness that all-thing has is He." [271] Therefore " He is in all-thing." " God doth all-thing, be it never so little. And nothing is done by hap nor by chance, but by the endless foresight of the wisdom of God." [272] But this is not pantheism : the foundation of all that exists and also of our being is God ; real, actual being belongs to God only, and yet the being of us His creatures is in itself not God, although it is in God.[273]

God creates all things—save evil and sin.[274] But evil and sin have no real existence. From the standpoint of the true, deeper, divine reality, of the divine life, they are not there. For this reason, Julian in her *Revelations* was unable to see sin : " For I believe," she says, " it has no manner of substance, nor part of being ; nor might be known but by the pains that it is cause of." [275] And at the close of her *Revelations*, after she has firmly convinced herself of the overwhelming, victorious and infinite power of God's love, she turns, filled with triumphant joy, to sin: " Ah, wretched sin, what art thou ? Thou are nought ! For I saw that God is all-thing. I saw not thee. And when I saw that God has made all-thing, I saw thee not. And when I saw that God does all-thing that is done, less and more, I saw thee not. And when I saw our Lord Jesus sit in our soul so worshipfully, and love and like and rule and guard all that He has made, I saw not thee." [276]

And yet in our imperfect, empiric world, evil, suffering and sin unquestionably exist, and are not only very really felt, but have an extremely important bearing on our spiritual life. This Julian knows very well and she is far from ignoring ; rather does she lay stress on their infinite importance and signi-ficance. Suffering cleanses and disciplines the soul ; but against sin we should, with God's help, fight unremittingly with all our strength, choosing rather any other suffering on earth or in the beyond.[277] The problem of evil and sin, the apparent con-tradiction between the true reality of things and their transient, empiric state, that problem, which Gregory of Nyssa, Augustine and Scotus Eriugena strove so hard to solve is, indeed, stated by Julian,[278] but she seeks no metaphysical explanation or solu-tion. She is only interested in what is necessary for our salvation, what immediately concerns it and what practically determines our spiritual condition, our relationship to God, our fellow-men and the world. " All that is beside our salvation is shut off from us and hidden." [279]

But the practical corollaries of this doctrine of the divine love as the basic element of the universe, of this recognition of God as the being, the immanent foundation and objective of the cosmic life, are very significant and are also observed by Julian. Like Francis she cannot bring herself to condemn the world as the kingdom of Satan. As we have seen, the world is for her a creation of the divine love, and has its root in the divine life. All that is good in the creature is God in His creation ; everything in the world, apart from sin, is brought to completion by the divine power, by God. The world is beautiful and filled with goodness. In the creation this love was manifested in all things and its highest revelation appeared in the redeeming sacrifice of Christ. And, exalted by this stream of love inundating the world, Julian loves and blesses the world, for in it she feels the presence of God. " He that generally loves his even-Christians," she says, " he loves all that is, and he that loves thus, he is safe. And thus will I love and thus I love." [280]

Dante was also a mystic. We see this in the nature of his love for Beatrice on the one hand, and on the other in the closing cantos of the " Paradiso."

Dante is overwhelmed by love, and he feels in love the presence of the divine.

> " Tanto gentile e tanto honesta pare
> La donna mia, quand'ella altrui saluta,
> Ch'ogni lingua devien tremando muta,
> E gli occhi non l'ardiscon di guardare.
>
> Ella si va, sentendosi laudare,
> Benignamente e d'umiltà vestuta ;
> E par che sia una cosa venuta
> Dal cielo in terra a miracol mostrare." *

---

* For English translation, see Note 281.

Many said after she had passed (Dante relates), "that is no woman but one of the fairest angels of heaven." And others said : "This is a wonder ; blessed be the Lord who is able to create so wondrously ! " [281] And for Dante himself she was revealed as "*un miracolo la cui radice . . . è solamente la mirabile Trinitade.*" [282]

That which had appeared to him in his earthly love, he also felt more comprehensively in the mystic experience to which the source of the conclusion of the " Paradiso " must be traced. One has only to listen to these deeply-felt mystical tones :

> " Da quinci innanzi il mio veder fu maggio
> Che il parlar nostro, ch'a tal vista cede
> E cede la memoria a tanto oltraggio

> . . . quasi tutta cessa
> Mia visione ed ancora mi distilla
> Nel cuor lo dolce che nacque da essa

> O abondante grazia, ond'io presunsi
> Ficcar lo viso per la luce eterna,
> Tanto che la veduta vi consunsi !

> La forma universal di questo nodo
> Credo, ch'io vidi, perchè più di largo,
> Dicendo questo, mi sento ch'io godo.

> O quanto è corto il dire, e come fioco.
> Al mio concetto ! e questo, a quel ch'io vidi,
> È tanto, che non basta a dicer poco. . . ."

Words are inadequate.

And lastly :

> " . . . la mia mente fu percossa
> Da un fulgore, in che sua voglia venne.
> All' alta fantasia quì mancò possa :
> Ma già volgeva il mio disiro e il ' velle,'
> Si come ruota che igualmente è mossa,
> L'Amor che muove il Sole e l'altre stelle." * [283]

Yes, these are mystic tones, the tones of a personal, tremendous, mystical experience. Through this experience the world and world phenomena are glorified for Dante.

> " La gloria di Colui, che tutto move
> Per l'universo penetra, e risplende
> In una parte più, e meno altrove."

Thus, as with a solemn organ peal—with the proclamation of God's splendour pervading the whole world and illuminating all things, he opens his "Paradiso." † [284] This beauty of God streams towards us out of all earthly beauty, the single real goal of our longing, even unknown to ourselves, is this divine beauty, this divine light :

> " . . . l'eterna luce
> Che vesta sola sempre amor accende ;
> E s'altra cosa vostro amor seduce
> Non è, se non di quella alcun vestigio
> Mal conosciuto, che quivi traluce." ‡ [285]

In the "Paradiso" the beauty of Beatrice is glorified for Dante as a reflection, an outpouring

---

* For English translation, see Note 283.
† For English translation, see Note 284.
‡ For English translation, see Note 285.

of the divine radiance—of the "*piacere eterno*"—therefore it cannot be reproduced or expressed, therefore he is overwhelmed by the radiance of her smile—the radiance of the divine light in her smile—"*Vincendo me col lume d'un sorriso.*" [286]

Dante was led by his love for Beatrice into this inward sanctuary; the stormy contradictions of his life were stilled. He felt himself suddenly gripped by a supernatural force, "moved" and borne—by the power of the love which rules the sun and the stars:

"L'Amor che muove il Sole e l'altre stelle!"

CHAPTER VI

THE TRANSFIGURATION OF THE WORLD AS EXPERI-
ENCED BY CHRISTIAN MYSTICS OF THE RENAIS-
SANCE AND OF MODERN TIMES

THE Renaissance period bears a very deep impress of the Platonic teaching, of the " degrees of love "— the rising of the soul from the beauty of individual things up to the source of beauty. The writings and utterances of the Renaissance Platonists are sometimes permeated by a certain mystical atmosphere, sometimes filled and warmed at the same time by a Christian spirit.[287]

The great Spanish mystic and poet, John of the Cross, sees (about the same time, *i.e.*, in the sixteenth century) in all creation " the footsteps of God "— for him the whole world is glorified by the beauty of the Beloved, *i.e.*, of the Incarnate Word, by the fact of His incarnation and " by the glory of His Resurrection in the body."

"As He walked through our woods"—we read in the mystical *Dialogue of the Soul with Christ her Bridegroom* —" He caused them, merely through the reflection of His countenance, to be clothed with His beauty " :—

> " Mil gracias derramando,
> Passò por estos sotos con presura ;
> Y yendolos mirando,
> Cod sola su figura
> Vestidos los dejò de su hermosura."

And the soul, " smitten with love through this trace of the beauty of her beloved which she found in creation," cries, " full of longing for His invisible beauty : Woe ! who can heal me ! " for all things on every side speak to her of His beauty and grace, and all this news, these messages of her Beloved which are scattered over the world, wound her mortally, but with unspeakable rapture :

> " . . . todos cuantos vagan
> De ti me van mil gracias refiriendo,
> Y todos mas me llagan
> Y déjame muriendo
> Un no sè què que queda balbuciendo." [288]

In the soul of the simple and humble Brother Lawrence of the Resurrection (a French mystic of the seventeenth century) the sight of a tree stripped of its leaves in winter awakens a sudden over-whelming, rapturous feeling, pervading the whole of life, of the infinite grace and power of God inundating the world.[289]

For now already, in this world, we are washed by the waves of eternity, by the streams of eternal life ; we already live in the eternity which was revealed to us in Jesus.

> " Du sprichst : Versetze dich aus Zeit in Ewigkeit :
> Ist denn an Ewigkeit und Zeit ein Unterscheid ? " *

cries Angelius Silesius.[290]

---

* " Thou speakest : transpose us from time unto eternity : is there then a difference between eternity and time ? "

For has anything at all an actual and real existence apart from the all-subduing, eternal life ?

" Man redt von Zeit und Ort, von Nun und Ewigkeit :
    Was ist denn Zeit und Ort, und Nun und Ewigkeit ? " * 291

Jacob Boehme said much the same two generations earlier :

> " Wem Zeit wie Ewigkeit
> Und Ewigkeit wie Zeit,
> Der ist befreit
> Von allem Streit." † 292

For Boehme the whole " external world with its substance is a covering of the spiritual world " 293 ; he feels the presence of God in all creatures, even in herbs and grasses.294 Already, now, " heaven pervades the whole world." 295 " Thou shalt therefore not think that the heavenly light in this world is extinguished in the spiritual sources of God : nay, it is no more than a darkness," which prevents us from seeing, " but did God remove the darkness which hovers over the light, and were thy eyes opened, thou shouldst see here also in this place where thou standest, sittest or liest in thy room, the beautiful face of God ; and all the gates of Heaven. . . ." 296 " This thou seest also in all God's works, how love hath poured itself into all things and is the most inward and outward foundation of all things. . . ." 297 That, O God, is " Thy inward spiritual kingdom

---

* " Men speak of time and place, of now and eternity : what then are time and place, and now and eternity ? "
† " To whom time is as eternity and eternity as time is freed from all strife."

as Thou dwellest in that which is hidden and fillest all Thy creatures and workest Thyself and doest all in all," Boehme wrote in his prayer-book shortly before his death.[298] But, at the same time, Boehme feels in the world not only the presence of God, but also the onslaught of the enemy forces, the powers of darkness, the terror of death and of hell. "The true heaven is everywhere in this present time until the last day, and the house of wrath, of hell and death, is also in this world, now, everywhere, until the last day." [299] The world is a great battle-field. For Christians there is unceasing strife and struggle, an endless stern battle with the powers of the evil one, with the "Prince of Darkness." For Boehme, therefore, a final glorification of the world is impending, at the end of time—the coming, supreme victory of life, the coming glorification of the creature and also of matter! " . . . Then will the earth, too, become crystalline, and the divine light will shine in all beings." [300] And for Jacob Boehme the centre-point and foundation of the whole process of world-glorification is the incarnation of the Son of God and His victory over death. This is an event of cosmic significance, the centre-point, the meaning and the driving force of the whole evolution of the world, the germ of immortality which is buried in the world.

For the German Romanticists, too (not uninfluenced by Boehme), the world is religiously, even mystically glorified, especially for the profoundest of them all—Novalis. We live "in a fairy world," and we ourselves know it not.[301] For him also this glorification of all reality is linked with the meek, loving figure of the Son of Man, the Son of God, who reconciled the earthly with the heavenly.[302]

Let us return to the world of the Christian East. The experiences of the old Oriental Fathers, those guides to the ascetic-mystical life, as they are collected in the *Philokalia*, spring into fresh life in that remarkable monument of Russian folk mysticism of the middle of the nineteenth century, which has already been mentioned, *The Candid Narratives of a Pilgrim told to his Confessor*. Exalted by the floods of abundant spiritual joy, he, too, feels himself a new, a different man and, like Simeon the New Theologian, contemplates the world with new eyes. For him, too, as for Isaac the Syrian, the world is ennobled and uplifted by the boundless love of Jesus which possesses his heart and pours itself over all creation. " At times I felt a burning love," the pilgrim relates, " for Jesus Christ and for all God's creation. At times sweet tears of thanks to the Lord streamed involuntarily from my eyes. At times a comforting warmth of the heart streamed through my whole frame and in rapture I felt all around me the presence of God." [303] And, again : " Not only in my inmost soul did I feel this, but also all outward things appeared to me in delightful form, and everything invited me to love and give thanks to God ; men, trees, plants, beasts—everything seemed so familiar, everywhere I found the imprint of the name of Jesus Christ." [304] All creatures testify to him " of the love of God for men, and everything yearns and sings praises to God. And I understood therefrom what in the *Dobrotolubie* (*Philokalia*) is called : ' understanding of the words of creation,' and I saw the way in which we can commune with God's creatures." [305]

And, in conclusion, there rises before us the figure of Russia's greatest writer, who has also drawn inspiration from the mystical streams of the Christian East. He is the most relentless portrayer of the horrors of life that has perhaps ever existed, the prober and painter of every disease, repulsive abnormality and deformity of the human soul, of the most terrifying depths of moral degeneracy, of the most appalling spiritual abysses, a man of " cruel talent," as he has been called by one critic, a tormentor of himself and of others, he who felt all the crushing burden and agony of pain and . . . shuddered—I mean Dostoievski! And yet he has found a way out, a solution of that most oppressive problem of suffering which never ceased to haunt him throughout his life—he found it in the incarnate God, in the living God, who descended into this vale of woe and shared our pain and thereby sanctified it! And in Dostoievski the cry of horror ceases with the triumphant glorification of the world and of life. This tone of jubilation and rapture crowns and rounds off his whole philosophy. Through the mouth of the aged Zosima he speaks " of the beauty of this world of God's and of His great mystery," " Truly all is beautiful and a source of wonder, for all is truth," and Christ is with all creatures. " How can it be otherwise, for the Word is truly for all things, the whole creation and every creature, every leaflet yearns towards the Word, praises God, mourns before Christ, and achieves this unconsciously through the mystery of its blameless life." " We alone are the godless and the stupid," cries Zosima, when still a youth, " and do not understand that life is a Paradise, for we need only try to understand, and immediately it is revealed to us in its full beauty we shall embrace one another and weep." [306]

Evil is, of course, too real for us to shut our eyes to it—that Dostoievski knows far better than anyone else—and yet suffering itself is glorified and becomes joy ! In the midst of the evil and sin reigning in the world, by which the soul is at times thrown into agonised bewilderment, " is given to us the mysterious, subconscious feeling of a living link with another world, a world higher and nobler." For " God took the seed out of the other worlds and sowed it in this earth and caused a garden to spring up ; and everything grew which could grow and that which grew lives and is living only through the consciousness of its contact with the mysterious other worlds." [307]

The soul of the mystics " thrills," like Dostoievski's, already now, already here on earth, already in this earthly environment, " as it touches the other worlds," in the consciousness of the divine nearness pervading all things, embracing and flooding the soul from all sides and glorifying it; and in this trembling it already, now, experiences in anticipation the coming complete glorification of the creature, the fulness of the revelation of the glory, that apogee of Christian hope : " That God may be all in all " ($\dot{o}$ $\theta\epsilon\dot{o}s$ $\pi\acute{a}\nu\tau a$ $\dot{\epsilon}\nu$ $\pi\hat{a}\sigma\iota\nu$).[308]

CHAPTER VII

THE TRANSFIGURATION OF THE WORLD AND OF LIFE IN THE EUCHARIST

But side by side with the personal mysticism of the great Christian heroes of the spirit we have also to examine more closely the collective mysticism of Christianity, which appears in the practice of the Church and especially in the Lord's Supper.

The glorification and sanctification of the earthly through the heavenly, this is the essential meaning of the Christian sacrament of the Eucharist. From the times of primitive Christianity the Lord's Supper has stood in the centre of the life of the community. The Eucharist is the vital nerve of the Church's life. To the faithful it is the most impressive and concrete realisation of the promise : " Lo, I am with you alway, even unto the end of the world." [309] The coming and the presence of the glorified Lord, the mystical representation and re-enactment of His death and resurrection, the revelation of a divine reality within the frame of the earthly being, the glorification through divine grace of the man and also of creation (already, now) and, lastly, the longing expectation of a complete revelation of the kingdom of glory to come—these are the fundamental experiences which have concentrated themselves in the sacrament of the Eucharist.

The presence of the Lord! While He was yet among His disciples Jesus promised them: "Where two or three are gathered together in My name there am I in the midst of them." [310] Even more concrete and realistic are the words as given in the sixth chapter of St John. And, lastly, at the culmination of His life on earth, immediately before the end—in the night before His Passion, Jesus gave to His disciples, while telling them of His approaching departure, His last and greatest "testament." For here at the Last Supper that which they took away with them as their inheritance from His whole life in common with them—the consciousness of unbroken communion with Him—finds its most concrete expression! In the primitive Church this feeling of communion is living, however living may also be the memory of that supreme act of their earthly life together; for it becomes the central act in the life of the community. "For I have received of the Lord that which also I delivered unto you, that the Lord Jesus the same night in which He was betrayed took bread; and when He had given thanks, He brake it, and said: 'Take, eat: This is My body, which is for you (broken for you), this do in remembrance of Me.' After the same manner also He took the cup, when He had supped, saying: 'This cup is the new testament in My blood: this do, as oft as ye drink it, in remembrance of Me,'" [311] and, similarly, in the Synoptic Gospels. And even in John, who gives no account of the Supper immediately before the Crucifixion, a similar note is sounded in Jesus' farewell to the disciples— the promise to be near them. He will come to them, He will remain with them, He will not desert them : "Yet a little while, and the world seeth Me no more ; but ye see Me : because I live, ye shall live also. In that day ye shall know that I am in My Father, and ye in Me, and I in you. He that hath My commandments and keepeth them, he it is that loveth Me : and he that loveth Me shall be loved of My Father, and I will love him, and will manifest Myself to him. . . . And My Father will love him, and we will come unto him, and make our abode with him." [312] And earlier in John's Gospel—after the miraculous feeding of the five thousand—we hear from the mouth of Jesus the much discussed words which run parallel in sense with the Synoptic accounts of the Last Supper : "Verily, verily, I say unto you . . . My flesh is meat indeed, and My blood is drink indeed. He that eateth My flesh and drinketh My blood dwelleth in Me, and I in him." [313]

This is not the place to examine closely these words of Jesus quoted by John and the corresponding words reported by the Synoptics. But one thing is clear : in this Lord's Supper, which is celebrated to His " memory," His nearness, His actual presence, is experienced by the faithful in a real, concrete and also mystical manner. It is in accordance with His revelation of Himself to the disciples at Emmaus as they brake bread. "And it came to pass, when He had sat down with them to meat, He took the bread, and blessed it, and brake, and gave to them. And their eyes were opened, and they knew Him ; and He vanished out of their sight." And they afterwards told the rest of the disciples " how He was known of them in the breaking of bread." [314] It is not without significance that two subsequent appearances of the risen, glorified Lord are connected with the taking of food.[315] This is the reason why " the breaking of bread " plays such a prominent part in the life of the primitive Church. They do it "with gladness and singleness of heart." [316] Paul is filled with the consciousness of the great mystery and awful sanctity of the action : " The cup of blessing which we bless, is it not the communion of the blood of Christ ? The bread which we break, is it not the communion of the body of Christ ? " " Wherefore whosoever shall eat this bread and drink this cup of the Lord unworthily, shall be guilty of the body and the blood of the Lord. But let a man examine himself, and so let him eat of that bread, and drink of that cup. For he that eateth and drinketh unworthily, eateth and drinketh damnation to himself, not discerning the Lord's body." [317] For the Lord is there. He is actually and truly there in His flesh and blood at the moment of the consummation of the mystery. This joyous rapture in the feeling of the presence of the Lord, of His coming near in the bread and wine of the Eucharist, permeates the closing words of the oldest eucharistic prayer that has come down to us (in the *Didache*) : " Let grace come and the world die away ! Hosannah to the God of David ! Whosoever is holy, let him approach ; whosoever is not, let him repent." And, finally, the closing cry quivering with joyous awe : *Maranatha* (" Come, our Lord ! ").[318]

This appeal in Aramaic takes us back to the earliest

period of the primitive Church in Jerusalem. We find it used already as a traditional formula by Paul (at the end of the first Epistle to the Corinthians), and from analogy with the *Didache* we may suppose that for Paul, too, it had an eucharistic meaning. "Greet ye one another with an holy kiss," Paul writes . . . "*Maranatha*" ("Come, O Lord"). [319] The same spirit also breathes in the eucharistic prayer of the "Acts of Thomas": "Come and enter into communion with us," [320] and in all Christian liturgies from the earliest onwards.

The centre-point of these old liturgies is the prayer for the coming of the Lord, for the descent of the Spirit or the Logos upon the eucharistic offerings, that they may be sanctified and become the body and blood of Christ. The *Anaphora Serapionis* (an Egyptian eucharistic prayer dating probably from the third century) runs : "Full is the heaven, full is also the earth of Thy glorious fame, O Lord of power ! Fill this sacrifice also with Thy power that we may partake of Thee." And again : "May Thy holy Word, O God of truth, descend upon this bread, that the bread may become the body of the Word ($\sigma\hat{\omega}\mu\alpha$ $\tau o\hat{v}$ $\lambda\acute{o}\gamma o\nu$) and upon this cup, that the cup may become the blood of truth ! " [321] The "Clementine" Liturgy (probably from Syria and in its present form dating probably from the end of the fourth century) . . . "We pray Thee, O Lord, that Thou send Thy Holy Spirit, the witness of the Passion of the Lord Jesus, upon this sacrifice, that He may make this bread the body of Thy Christ ($\mathring{\alpha}\pi o\phi\acute{\eta}\nu\eta$) and this cup the blood of Thy

Christ." [322]   Still older is the invocation of the Holy Ghost in the eucharistic prayers of the Church preserved for us (in Ethiopian and Latin) in the "Egyptian Church Ordinances," which bear the impress of great antiquity. " We beseech Thee to send down Thy Holy Spirit upon this oblation of the Church, that . . . Thou mayest grant to those who partake of it that they be made holy and be filled with the Holy Spirit." [323]   This prayer for the sanctification of the eucharistic elements through the Holy Spirit, and for the descent of the Holy Spirit, becomes the fundamental and essential constituent, not only of all Eastern liturgies, but also of the early liturgies of the West. (In the West, *i.e.*, in the Roman Liturgy, the invocation of the Holy Spirit completely lost its importance later and has almost disappeared. [324])   " Send down Thy most Holy Spirit, O Lord, upon us and upon these holy offerings," says the old Greek Liturgy of St James (in its present form not later than the beginning of the fifth century). [325]   There are similar invocations of the Holy Spirit in the Liturgies of St Basil, of St John Chrysostom, and indeed in all the Eastern liturgies.   And in one of the old Eastern rituals of the Eucharist is found : " We beseech Thy Majesty, O Lord, that the fulness of Thy divinity may descend upon this bread and this cup." [326] All these fervent supplications of the Church have their source in that earliest of eucharistic prayers : "Come, O Lord " (*Maranatha*). " Be Thou present in our midst, O Jesus, Thou gracious High Priest," says the West Gothic Liturgy of the 5th-6th century, " as Thou wert in the midst of Thy disciples, and bless this oblation" . . . (" *Adesto, adesto, Jesu bone pontifex, in medio nostro, sicut fuisti in medio discipulorum tuorum ; et sanctifica hanc oblationem* ").[327]   And, similarly, in the Ethiopian Liturgy : "We beseech and pray Thee, O Lord, that Thou mayst be with us at this hour ; reveal unto us Thy countenance, be with us and in our midst." [328]

Christ's nearness, His coming, is anticipated— hence that mood of exaltation, that upward surge of the spirit with which the eucharistic prayers are offered. For they are born out of the charismatic spirit, out of the charismatic thanksgiving prayers of the primitive Church. "Lift up your hearts ! "— "We lift them up unto the Lord."—" Let us give thanks unto the Lord ! "—" It is meet and right . . .," etc. (Ἄνω τὰς καρδίας. —Ἔχομεν πρὸς τὸν κύριον.—Εὐχαριστήσωμεν τῷ κυρίῳ—Ἄξιον καὶ δίκαιον . . . .) So it is already in the oldest liturgical monuments of the third and fourth centuries that have come down to us.[329] And the liturgist then begins the great prayer of the offering, elevation —ἀναφορά—of the sacrifices and of the heart, the prayer in which the piety of the early Church finds its noblest expression. This " anaphoristic " prayer concludes, as is well known, with a remembrance of the Last Supper of Jesus, with repetition aloud of the sacramental words and the subsequent invocation of the Holy Spirit, its first part being a hymn of thanksgiving and praise : " It is meet and right to praise and glorify Thee the unborn Father of the only-begotten Son Jesus Christ," occurs in one of the oldest of the " anaphoristic " prayers (the Egyptian Anaphora of Bishop Serapion) . . . " we praise

Thee, invisible Father, giver of immortality. Thou art the source of life, the source of light, the source of all grace and all truth. . . . Thou that pardonest all and raisest all to Thee through the manifestation of Thy beloved Son. We beseech Thee make us living men, give us the spirit of light that we may behold Thee the true God and Him whom Thou hast sent, Jesus Christ! Give us the Holy Spirit that we may utter and proclaim Thy unspeakable mysteries. May the Lord Jesus speak in us and the Holy Spirit praise Thee through us. For Thou art high above all dominion and might and power. . . . Before Thee stand thousands upon thousands and ten thousands upon ten thousands of angels, arch-angels, thrones, dominions, principalities and powers, before Thee stand the six-winged seraphim " . . . and similarly in the later liturgies. It is the moment of highest tension for the religious mind expectant of the Lord.

At last the great mystery is consummated and with awe and joy the faithful bow themselves before the present Lord. As in the prayer of the old *Didache*, we hear once more the exultant cry, with which is greeted and received the Lord appearing in the eucharistic elements. " Honour be to God in the highest and peace upon earth and good-will towards men! Hosannah to the Son of David, praised be He that cometh in the name of the Lord, the Lord God hath appeared to us, Hosannah in the highest!" cries the Liturgy of St Clement [330]; " . . . For behold the King of Honour entereth," says the Byzantine Mass, of the pre-consecrated offerings, " . . . behold the mysterious sacrifice, it is consummated and is brought in in splendour. Let us draw near in faith and love, that we may become partakers of eternal life, Hallelujah." But usually this greeting of the King of Honour comes earlier, before the consecration of the eucharistic elements. On the one hand in the angels' cry of the "anaphoristic" prayer: "Holy, Holy, Holy, Lord God of Sabaoth . . . Hosannah in the highest, praised be He that cometh in the name of the Lord! Hosannah in the highest." (Only in the Liturgy of St Clement do we find this cry following the transubstantiation and immediately preceding the reception of the Sacrament.) Then in the hymns which accompany the bearing of the eucharistic offerings prepared for consecration from the sacrificial table to the High Altar: "Let all human flesh be silent" says the old Greek Liturgy of St James (this hymn is now sung only once in the year, in the Liturgy of St Basil on Holy Saturday, when it replaces the usual Song of the Cherubim) "and stand in fear and trembling, and let there be no thought of earthly things, for the King of Kings and Lord of Lords cometh to be sacrificed and to offer Himself as food for them that believe. . . ." And, similarly, in the usual Song of the Cherubim of the Byzantine Mass (originating in Constantinople in the sixth century): " . . . Let us now lay aside all earthly care that we may receive the King of all, who is accompanied by the invisible choirs of angels. Hallelujah!" [331]

The angels join the faithful at the consummation of the great mystery; unseen, adoring and trembling the hosts of heaven stand (" now the unseen heavenly hosts serve with us ").[332] The faithful are exalted into another sphere of life; here on earth is anticipated the kingdom of eternity, the fulness of God's presence. "Christ is among us!" cry the celebrant priests one to the other as they exchange the kiss of peace and answer one another: "He it is and will be!" (in the Liturgies of St Basil and of St John Chrysostom). "Thus art Thou glorified and dwellest among men, not to burn them with fire but to lighten them," says the eucharistic prayer of one of the Syrian Masses. The Armenian ritual (of Byzantine origin) says, like the Byzantine: "Christ hath appeared among us. . . ." And, again: "Ye that are present at the Holy Supper of the King behold Christ the King sitting upon the throne surrounded by the hosts of heaven." [333] The veil is drawn back (in a number of old liturgies [334]), the gates of heaven open. [335] "Let us stand in fear and trembling, in humility and holiness," says the ancient ritual of the Syrian Liturgy of St James, "for the sacrifice is consummated and the glory is revealed (*et majestas exoritur*). The gate of heaven openeth and the Holy Ghost descendeth upon these holy mysteries, penetrating them. We stand in a place of awe and fear together with the Cherubim and Seraphim; we have become the brothers and fellow-servants of the angels, and together with them we perform the service of the Fire and Spirit." [336]

But the mysterious coming and the glorious presence of the Lord, radiant in splendour and surrounded by the angel choirs, do not constitute the whole experience of the faithful in the liturgy. One note is, and remains fundamental and decisive: "Ye proclaim the Lord's death till He come." [337]

His death and crucifixion are lived through again as an overwhelming, ever-present, ever-living reality. The whole Christian " philosophy of salvation " is here focused as in a burning-glass. Glorification of the earthly, new, divine life-force, eternal life appearing in the midst of our earthly existence ; and all this solely and alone through His death, His crucifixion and His Passion, through the " foolishness of the Cross " and humiliation ; for without this there is no eternal life. The " memory " of His death continually re-experienced, the mystically real re-enactment of the sacrifice of Golgotha is the vital nerve of the whole eucharistic Sacrament, for the " new covenant " was made " in His blood." Like Paul, the apologist Justin says of the Eucharistic Supper of the Christians that it brings to mind the suffering which the Son of God has suffered for them.[338] " The Lord's Passion is the sacrifice we offer," says Cyprian.[339]

The whole liturgy, it may be said, is contained in these thoughts. In the Greek *Proscomidia* (introductory part of the Mass) we find : " The Lamb of God is slain, who beareth the sin of the world, for the life and salvation of the world. . . ." " Let all human flesh be silent," proclaims, as we have seen, the old Liturgy of St James, while the eucharistic elements were being borne from the sacrificial table to the altar : " for the King of Kings and the Lord of Lords cometh to be sacrificed." One of the established features of the " anaphoristic " prayers has been from the earliest times the so-called *Anamnese*— the solemn and impressive recital of the Passion and resurrection of the incarnate God.[340] Thus we read in the liturgy of the Veronese fragment of the old Church Ordinances : " *Memores igitur mortis et resurrectionis eius offerimus tibi panem et calicem, gratias tibi agentes.*" [341]   The recital of the redeeming Passion of Christ is given with unusual fulness in the ancient Coptic Liturgy of Saint Gregory : " Thou hast suffered the scorn of the godless," says the priest, " Thou hast offered Thy back to the scourge and Thy cheeks to blows ; but for my sake, O Lord, Thou hast not turned away Thy face from the shame of the spitting." The people : "Have mercy, O Lord ! " The priest : " Thou camest like a lamb to the slaughter ; even to the very Cross Thou didst show Thy care for me ; my sins hast Thou slain through Thy burial ; Thou hast risen unto heaven, the firstfruits of my being. . . ." [342]   And after the introductory words the priest, in a number of ancient Eastern Masses, adds the words that are placed in the mouth of the Lord Himself and are inspired by Paul's Epistle to the Corinthians : " As often as ye eat this bread and drink this cup ye do show My death and acknowledge My resurrection and think upon Me till I come." [343]   And the people answer : "We proclaim Thy death and acknowledge Thy resurrection." [344]   In a word, the Lamb of God offering Himself willingly for the sacrifice stands in the centre of the whole liturgy.[345]   And at the same time this suffering Lord is also the living, the glorified and the risen Lord, and the whole Eucharist is illumined by the radiance of His glory, the radiance of His resurrection.

Thus it is not only that His presence is felt, but His Passion and glorification are also experienced anew. It is now easy to understand that feeling of awe and trembling, that feeling of the great holiness of the awful mystery—a mystery of universal, cosmic significance, that permeates the liturgies : " Let us stand in seemly fashion, let us stand in awe, let us be watchful to perform the holy sacrifice in peace ! " [346] The Alexandrian Liturgy proclaims, after the consummation of the mystery : " The mystery is accomplished. We thank Thee, O Lord God, almighty Father, that Thy grace unto us is great, and that Thou hast prepared for us that upon which the angels thirst to look." [347] One of the old liturgies—the Syrian Mass of St James—lays particular stress upon this feeling of trembling and awe before the face of the mystery. Over and over again the deacon summons the congregation to attention and reverence : " Now is the time of fear, it is the awful hour. The heavenly powers stand in fear and serve Him trembling. . . . It is the hour when the sacrifice of redemption is accomplished and sin flees before Him. Servants of the Church, tremble, for ye are partakers of the living fire. The power bestowed upon you is more splendid than that of the Seraphim. Blessed is the soul of him that standeth in the church in purity, for the Holy Spirit writeth its name and raiseth it unto heaven. Deacons, be filled with trembling at this holy time when the Holy Spirit descendeth to sanctify the souls of them that receive this into themselves. . . . The powers of heaven stand with us in the holy place and serve the body of the Son of God, who is slain in our presence. Approach and receive from Him forgiveness of sins. Hallelujah ! " [348] Similarly, this trembling of the creature before the inexpressible mystery is emphasised by some of the Fathers of the Church, especially by St John Chrysostom [349] and the Syrian ecclesiastical writers.[350] In the East Syrian Liturgy the celebrant speaks for himself in the "anaphoristic" prayer : "Woe is me ! woe is me ! who am seized with trembling, for I am a man of unclean lips and dwell among a people of unclean lips, and my eyes have seen the King, the mighty Lord ! How fearful is this place to-day ! Here is no other than the house of God and the gates of heaven ; for eye to eye hast Thou allowed us to look upon Thee, O Lord. But now let Thy grace be with us. . . . Honour be to Thy mercy, for Thou hast united the earthly with the heavenly." [351]

The separating partition has fallen with His death and resurrection ! Therefore in a number of liturgies, as we have seen, the curtain is pulled aside (just as the veil in the Temple at Jerusalem was rent in twain) : "No one is bound ; let all dare to approach these mysteries ; for the veil is removed and grace and mercy are poured out abundantly." [352]

But there is yet more. Not only is the actual presence of the crucified and glorified Lord experienced by the faithful in the Eucharist, but their own being is glorified and they become partakers of His glorified, eternal life as they assimilate Him spiritually and physically in His body and blood. The words : "Take, eat," "drink ye all of this," are the climax of the eucharistic rite. And this assimilation of His flesh and blood bind us to Him organically. Already in St John we find the words : "He that eateth My flesh and drinketh My blood, dwelleth

in Me, and I in him." [353]   Man becomes a partaker
of His body, his mortal nature is glorified. "He
that eateth Me, even he shall live by Me. He that
eateth My flesh and drinketh My blood hath eternal
life ; and I will raise him up at the last day." . . .
And, similarly, the earliest eucharistic prayer of the
Christian community that has come down to us (from
the *Didache*) : "Thou, Lord, ruler of all . . .
gavest men food and drink that they might thank
Thee and gavest us spiritual food and drink and
eternal life through Thy Servant (Son)." [354]

Ignatius of Antioch speaks of the bread of
the Eucharist as a "physic of immortality
($\phi \acute{a} \rho \mu a \kappa o \nu$ $\dot{a} \theta a \nu a \sigma \acute{\iota} a s$), as an antidote preventing death
($\dot{a} \nu \tau \acute{\iota} \delta o \tau o s$ $\tau o \hat{v}$ $\mu \grave{\eta}$ $\theta a \nu \epsilon \hat{\iota} \nu$), but ensuring continuance
of life in Jesus Christ." [355]   How could our
flesh, says Irenæus, not partake of eternal life "since
it is nourished by the flesh and blood of the Lord
and is a member of His body ? "   "Our bodies,
partaking of the Eucharist, are no longer corruptible,
since they have hope in the resurrection unto
eternity." [356]   "In the form of bread the body is
given to thee and in the form of wine the blood,"
Cyril of Jerusalem instructs the newly-baptised
Christians in the mysteries of the faith, "that, partaking of the body and the blood of Christ, thou
mayest become one body and one blood with Him
($\ddot{\iota} \nu a$ $\gamma \acute{\epsilon} \nu \eta$ . . . $\sigma \acute{v} \sigma \sigma \omega \mu o s$ $\kappa a \grave{\iota}$ $\sigma \acute{v} \nu a \iota \mu o s$ $a \dot{v} \tau o \hat{v}$). And
in such-wise we also become bearers of Christ,
for His body and His blood spread through our
limbs ($\tau o \hat{v}$ $\sigma \acute{\omega} \mu a \tau o s$ $a \dot{v} \tau o \hat{v}$ $\kappa a \grave{\iota}$ $\tau o \hat{v}$ $a \ddot{\iota} \mu a \tau o s$ $\epsilon \dot{\iota} s$ $\tau \grave{a}$
$\dot{\eta} \mu \acute{\epsilon} \tau \epsilon \rho a$ $\dot{a} \nu a \delta \iota \delta o \mu \acute{\epsilon} \nu o \upsilon$ $\mu \acute{\epsilon} \lambda \eta$). In such-wise, according to St Peter, we become ' partakers of the divine

nature.' " [357] "Christ the slain," writes Athanasius, in his Easter epistles, "giveth Himself freely to all, and, dwelling in each one, becometh in him the source of the water which floweth into eternal life." [358] "The spirit in Thy bread, the fire in Thy wine are quite new wonders received by our lips," exclaims Ephraem Syrus in wonderment. "To creatures of the flesh the Lord giveth to taste of the fire and of the spirit. . . . Ye taste of the fire, which is in the bread, and receive life." [359] In the Eucharist "the Lord uniteth Himself with the bodies of the faithful, that through union with the immortal, man, too, may reach immortality," writes Gregory of Nyssa.[360] Many other similar utterances of the Fathers of the Church could be quoted.[361]

The liturgies also, from the earliest onwards, say the same thing. The Eucharist feeds the "hope of eternal life," as the liturgical papyrus of Der-Balyzeh says,[362] it is the "physic of life" ($\phi \acute{a} \rho \mu a \kappa o \nu$ $\zeta \omega \hat{\eta} s$) as the "Anaphora Serapionis" puts it.[363] May it become for those who receive it "health for their souls and life for their bodies in Thy living world" (prayer from the Acts of Thomas [364]), "forgiveness of sins and great hope of the resurrection of the dead and new life in the Kingdom of Heaven" (from the old East Syrian Liturgy of Adai and Mari [365]). The reception of the Sacrament sanctifies soul, body and spirit, we become $\sigma \acute{v} \sigma \sigma \omega \mu o \iota$ $\kappa a \grave{\iota} \sigma o \mu \mu \acute{\epsilon} \tau o \chi o \iota \kappa a \grave{\iota} \sigma \acute{v} \mu \mu o \rho \phi o \iota \tau o \hat{v} \chi \rho \iota \sigma \tau o \hat{v} \sigma o \upsilon$ (in the prayer of the "bowing of the head" in the Alexandrian Liturgy of St Basil).[366] In the communion prayers of the Greek Church we read among other things : "May Thy holy body become for me the bread of eternal life, O merciful Lord, and Thy sacred blood the healing of many diseases. Trembling, I receive the fire that I may not be consumed like wax and grass. O awful mystery ! O mercy of God ! How can I, filth that I am, receive the divine body and blood and become incorruptible ? " [367]

But this is no merely external " magical," partaking by man of the divine being, independently of moral circumstances. The efficacy of the Sacrament is inextricably bound up with the moral life of the man. Only such as are morally cleansed, only the holy, are worthy to approach the Holy. " Let the man examine himself now, and then let him eat of this bread, and drink of this cup. For he that eateth and drinketh unworthily, eateth and drinketh damnation to himself, not discerning the Lord's body," Paul writes to the Corinthians. [368] " If a man be holy, he may approach, if not, let him repent," says the *Didache*. [369]

The Lord's Supper must be received in the spirit of brotherly love. Ignatius urges that the Eucharist should be consummated in peace and unity. [370] Justin speaks of the kiss of peace which the faithful exchange before the completion of the eucharistic rite. [371] All liturgies, beginning with the oldest, mention this kiss of peace, which is undoubtedly of apostolic origin. For example we find in the Liturgy of St Clement " Ἀσπάσασθε ἀλλήλους ἐν φιλήματι ἁγίῳ." [372] The Armenian rite explains the meaning of this kiss of peace as follows : " Peace is proclaimed, the Church has become one spirit ; the kiss is given as a bond of complete unity ; enmity is set aside and love has covered all things." [373] Side by side with this emphasis of the necessity for brotherly concord, all liturgies, both Eastern and Western, new and old, are pervaded by fervent prayer for the moral purification of the faithful, particularly of the celebrants, that they may be made worthy to witness the mystery and to receive the awful and holy Sacrament " without damnation."

In the Greek Liturgy of St James, the celebrant cries before the sanctification of the eucharistic offerings : " Show us these holy gifts in radiant light, fill the eyes of our spirit with endless light, cleanse our minds of all blemish of the flesh and of the spirit and make them worthy of this awful, fear-awakening presence ! " [374] Or, in the Byzantine Mass of St Basil : " Cleanse us of all blemish both of the flesh and of the spirit and teach us to perform the holy sacrifice in Thy fear, that, partaking of Thy sacrament in purity of conscience, we may be united with the sacred body and blood of Thy Christ, and, receiving it worthily, may have Christ dwelling in our hearts and become temples of the holy spirit. . . ." [375]

From all sides, from all the liturgies, this ceaseless unwearying cry rings out to us—the prayer for purity, moral rebirth, sanctification of life and of soul. That is the underlying spirit, the warp, the all-dominating, powerful characteristic of the eucharistic ritual.

This partaking of the Sacrament was regarded from the earliest times as a fount of moral strength, as a powerful means of grace on the way to the moral renewal of man.[376] The oldest eucharistic prayers ask for " holiness and penetration by the Holy Spirit," [377]

for increase of faith ($\pi\rho\sigma\theta\acute{\eta}\kappa\eta$ $\pi\acute{\iota}\sigma\tau\epsilon\omega\varsigma$),[378] for
" strengthening of every virtue " [379] as results of the
Communion, " that it may not bring us to judgment
and damnation, but to a renewal of the soul, the
body and the spirit." [380] We must take Christ
into ourselves, " into our breasts to subdue the
passions of our flesh," writes Clement of Alexandria.
" They who in faith partake " of the Eucharist, " are
sanctified in both body and soul." [381] This prayer
for a dual, physical and spiritual effect of the
Eucharist, and for the moral glorification of man
appears with special force and emphasis in a later
prayer of the Eastern Church (that of Simeon
Metaphrastes, of the tenth century—the third of the
thanksgiving prayers following the Communion) :
" Thou that hast willingly offered me Thy flesh for
my nourishment, Thou, a fire consuming the unworthy, consume me not, O my Creator ! Rather
penetrate all my limbs and bones, and inmost
being, and my heart ! Consume the thorns of all
my misdeeds ! Purify my soul and sanctify my
mind and strengthen my joints and bones. Brighten
my five senses. Nail me wholly to Thy fear. Shield
me always, guard and protect me from every deed
and word that bringeth damnation to the soul.
Cleanse, wash and adorn me ; make me better ; and
teach and enlighten me. Make of me the dwelling-
place only of Thy spirit, and let me no more be
the dwelling-place of sin, that, after I have become
Thy dwelling through the entrance of Thy supper,
every fiend and every passion may shun me like
fire. . . ." [382]

As we see, a new life is beginning, a life fed by the

reception of the Lord in the eucharistic offerings, and at the same time the body is spiritualised and receives the germ of glorification and of eternal life.

But already, in the faith of the ancient Church, the significance of the Eucharist transcends its effect upon the individual man ; for its meaning is a cosmic, mystical re-enactment of the sacrifice of Golgotha. Here the earthly is reconciled to the heavenly— says Ignatius of Antioch : " οὐδέν ἐστιν ἄμεινον εἰρήνης, ἐν ᾗ πᾶς πόλεμος καταργεῖται ἐπουρανίων καὶ ἐπιγείων." [383] For Irenæus the eucharistic gifts—the bread and wine which are offered to God and which become the flesh and blood of Christ—are symbols of all visible nature, firstfruits of the creation : "We offer to God His own and accordingly we proclaim the communion and union of the flesh and spirit." For " the earthly bread is, after the invocation of God has been spoken over it, no longer ordinary bread, but hath become the Eucharist, which is composed of two elements—the earthly and the heavenly " (ὁ ἀπὸ τῆς γῆς ἄρτος προσλαβόμενος τὴν ἐπίκλησιν τοῦ θεοῦ, οὐκέτι κοινὸς ἄρτος ἐστὶν, αλλ' εὐχαριστια, ἐκ δύο πραγμάτων συνεστηκυῖα, ἐπιγείου τε καὶ οὐρανίον). [384] By the sanctification of the bread and wine, the firstfruits of visible creation, to become the body and blood of Christ, all visible nature is potentially sanctified. For " He hath acknowledged the cup taken from creation to be His own blood . . . and declared the bread taken out of creation to be undoubtedly and surely His own body." " The vine," continues Irenæus, " sunk in the earth brings forth fruits in its season, and the grain of corn, fallen in the earth and dissolved, springs up manifold through the omnipotent breath of God; but then (both) through the wisdom of God come to man's use and, by taking into themselves God's Word they become the Eucharist, which is the body and blood of Christ. And so our bodies fed thereon shall, after their burial and dissolution in the earth, rise in their time as the Word of God grants them resurrection to the honour of God the Father. . . ." [385] Therefore " our teaching " (that the matter is not in itself evil and that the flesh shall rise again) " accords with the Eucharist and the Eucharist gives strength to our teaching." [386] And for Ephraim the Syrian the Eucharist constitutes a rehabilitation of matter. The Lord intended to show through the breaking of bread, " that He did not put on an unclean body. . . ." [387]

Similar ideas—glorification of the creature in connection with the Lord's Supper—also pervade the rites of the old liturgies. The old Sabbath service of the Jewish synagogue is full of praise of the Lord for the creation of the world, merging into thanksgiving for His beneficence towards the chosen race. In their external form the eucharistic prayers of the Christian liturgies are connected with these prayers of the old synagogues. [388] They, too, begin with the glorification of God's creative activity and with an account of His leading of the human race under the old covenant. But they have their centre in the fundamental fact of the whole history of the world—the incarnation, the path of life, the Passion, the crucifixion and the resurrection of the Son of God and in the institution of the Eucharist Sacrament through Him, " in the night when He was betrayed." "The eye sharpened by religion," writes Father Odo Casel, the sensitive investigator of the liturgical life of the Early Church, "now perceived the whole earthly temporality in a different light. Creation assumed a new meaning since it received an objective and focus in Christ. . . ." [389] The praise of God's act of creation in the eucharistic prayers is therefore not merely an inheritance from the past, a continuation of inherited rites, but grows organically, by the force of an inherent necessity, out of the whole spirit and philosophy of primitive Christianity, out of its completely new, overwhelming and joyously astounding apprehension of the history of the world as the process of redemption, glorification and restoration to God of the creature. The deepest need of the primitive Church found appropriate expression in thanking God for all His mercies towards creation, which now received in the fulness of time its crowning and consummation, in the appearance in the world and incarnation of the Son. It now becomes clear to us why a great part of the oldest eucharistic prayers of Christianity cede so important a place to the mention of God's creation ; for all things, including this creation itself, receive a new spiritualised meaning and worth when viewed from that central point, that apex of the world process upon which the faithful —" in Christ "—feel themselves to be.

The eucharistic prayer of the *Didache* says : " Thou, all-powerful Lord, hast created all things for Thy name's sake. . . ." [390] In the middle of the fourth century Cyril of Jerusalem describes as follows the liturgies of the time : " Thereafter " (*i.e.*, after the beginning of the eucharistic prayer) "we think of heaven and earth and the sea, the sun and the moon, the stars and all creation, both reasoning and un-reasoning, of the visible and invisible, of the angels, archangels, powers, dominions, principalities, author-ities, of the throne, of the multiform cherubim, and we repeat with emphasis the words of David, ' Glorify the Lord with me ! ' " [391] All creation is summoned to take part in the praise of God. And in the vision of the New Testament Apocalypse we hear : " In the midst of the throne and of the four beasts, and in the midst of the elders, stood a Lamb as it had been slain . . .," and they all fell down before the Lamb saying : " Worthy is the Lamb that was slain to receive power and riches, and wisdom, and strength, and honour, and glory, and blessing. And every creature which is in heaven, and on the earth, and under the earth, and such as are in the sea, and all that are in them, heard I saying, Blessing, and honour, and glory, and power, be unto Him that sitteth upon the throne, and unto the Lamb for ever and ever ! . . ." [392]

In the first epistle of Clement (end of the first century) we find a long hymn of praise, which, in the opinion of investigators, bears a definite " cultic " character and is perhaps connected with the euchar-istic Sacrament. [393] And the Liturgy of St Clement (fourth century, apparently of Syrian origin) gives in its eucharistic prayer an especially developed description of the divine work of creation :

" Thou art He that hast created the heavens as a chamber and spread it like a leathern cover through Thy will alone, that hast fixed the firmament and created night and day and hast brought the light out of Thy treasure chamber . . . and sent the darkness for the refreshment of the beasts which move upon the earth, that hast set the sun in the heaven to rule over the day and the moon to rule over the night and hast ordered the choir of stars in the heavens to praise Thy glory ; that hast made the water for drinking and cleansing, the life-giving air for inbreathing and outbreathing, . . . that hast created fire to lighten the darkness, to comfort our need, to warm and lighten us ; Thou that hast divided the great sea from the earth . . . and filled it with great and small beasts, and filled the earth with tame and wild beasts, and crowned it with grasses and adorned it with flowers and en-riched it with seeds ; Thou that hast firmly estab-lished the abyss and surrounded it with a great wall, with heaped-up seas of salt water, and made it fast with gates of finest sand . . . ; that hast engirdled this world created by Thy Christ with rivers, watered it with streams and drenched it with eternal springs and set it about with mountains that the foundations of the earth may be unshakable !

" For Thou hast filled and adorned Thy world with sweet-smelling and healing herbs, with many and divers beasts, stronger and weaker, useful for food or labour, with tame and wild things, with the hiss of creeping beasts, with the voices of manifold birds, also with the circling of the years, the succession of the months and days, the chain of the changing winds, the course of the clouds which pour down rain for the nourishment of the fruits and the sustenance of the life of the beasts and for the increase of the herbs and plants. . . ." We are reminded of the inspired praise of the creation and the writings of the Old Testament—particularly in the Book of Job or in the Psalm of Creation with which the whole tone, as well as some of the literal quotations, are connected. For the rest, in the other eucharistic prayer, all this part is considerably shorter and sometimes entirely wanting. In the Greek Liturgy of St James, for example, there is merely : " The Heavens praise Thee, and their whole might, the sun, the moon and all the choir of stars, the earth, the sea and all that therein is, the heavenly Jerusalem, the church of the first-born that stands written upon the heavens, the angels and archangels," etc.[394]

" For Thou hast created the heavens and all that is in the heavens," the celebrant prays in the " Anaphora " of the Liturgy of St Mark, " the earth and all that is upon the earth, the sea, the tides, the rivers and all that therein is, and hast created man in Thy image." [395]

But in the Christian liturgies all this is merely introductory to the re-enactment in the Eucharist of the supreme event of the world's history, already potentially glorifying creation and causing creation to partake already of incorruptibility, the incarnation and crucifixion of the Logos. Thus, for example, the Egyptian Liturgy of St Mark proclaims, immediately before the consecration of the eucharistic gifts : " Verily, heaven and earth are full of Thy glory through the coming of our Lord and God and Saviour Jesus Christ " ($\delta\iota\acute{a}$ $\tau\hat{\eta}\varsigma$ $\dot{\epsilon}\pi\iota\varphi\alpha\nu\epsilon\acute{\iota}\alpha\varsigma$ $\tau o\hat{v}$ $\kappa\nu\rho\acute{\iota}o\nu$ $\kappa\alpha\iota$ $\theta\epsilon o\hat{v}$ $\kappa\alpha\grave{\iota}$ $\sigma\omega\tau\hat{\eta}\rho o\varsigma$ $\dot{\eta}\mu\hat{\omega}\nu$ $I\eta\sigma o\hat{v}$ $X\rho\iota\sigma\tau o\hat{v}$).[396] For,

" through the Passion of Thy incarnate Son all creatures are renewed and man has again become immortal, clothed in a garment which none can steal from him," are the introductory words of the Armenian Mass.[397] And, again, in the eucharistic prayer : " It pleased Him to take up His abode among us, in the flesh which He received from the virgin, and like a divine architect He has built a new creation, making of the earth heaven." We meet with the same thought in the Syrian Liturgy of St James in the prayer which introduces the censing : " We pray Thee . . ., O blessed Root that hast blossomed out of the thirsting earth—out of Mary—and that hast filled all creation with the fragrance of Thy wondrous sweetness." [398] In a manuscript fragment of an old eucharistic prayer of the Persian Church we read : " Over all creation has grace spread . . . has grace been poured out." " All is Thine, and us as well as all creatures hast Thou made Thine. . . ." [399]

Round this central point—the consecration of the eucharistic sacrifice—which is of general, nay, cosmic significance, are concentrated the fervent supplications of the congregation ; for the entire Holy Church, for all brothers, living and dead, and also for the visible creation.[400] " We pray and beseech Thee, Thou gracious Lover of man," is, for instance, the prayer of the Liturgy of St Mark, " remember, O Lord, Thy one, holy, universal and apostolic Church which extends from end to end of the earth ; remember all nations and Thy whole flock. Pour into our hearts heavenly peace and vouchsafe to us peace in this life." Then follows the prayer for all those set in authority and for the whole nation, for all who are sick, suffering and oppressed; for all who are in trouble and for travellers. " But keep, O Lord, our journey through this life free also from storm and hurt unto the end. Send down refreshing rain upon the places that have need of it; gladden and renew through it the face of the earth, that it may delight in the refreshing drops and become green. . . . Water the furrows of the earth and multiply their fruits. Bless, O Lord, the fruits of the earth, keep them for us free from disease and hurt, and prepare them for our sowing and our harvest. . . . Bless now also, O Lord, the crown of the year through Thy goodness for the sake of the poor among Thy people, for the sake of the widow and the orphan, for the sake of the wanderer and the new-comer and for the sake of us all who trust in Thee and call upon Thy Holy name." [401]

Similar prayers also exist in other liturgies of the Egyptian type,[402] and in the Liturgy of St Clement,[403] in the Syrian Mass of St James,[404] and others that are based upon it,[405] in the ritual of the Ethiopian Church [406] and in the Byzantine Liturgy of St Basil.[407] A long prayer for the living and the dead immediately following the consummation of the eucharistic sacrifice is common to all liturgies, both Western and Eastern, though the visible creation is not always mentioned in these intercessions. (They are absent, for instance, from the Liturgy of St Chrysostom and from the Roman Mass canon.) We are thus involuntarily reminded of the experiences of the mediæval mystic Heinrich Suso, which we have already described: how in the moment

when he proclaimed the *sursum corda* in the Mass
" the loving arms of the soul were lifted up and
stretched outwards towards the countless number of
created things "—and in thought he gathered all
creatures around him before the eucharistic altar.[408]

And so we see man and nature are glorified in the
Sacrament of the Lord's Supper. The spirit of
communion here finds its expression, the bond of
brotherhood organically uniting in an act of prayer
and praise all the faithful, both the living and the
departed, and the whole Church, heavenly and
earthly, and—what is more—the whole of creation
gathers round " the head of the body, the Church :
who is the Beginning, the first - born from the
dead,[409] the Prince of Life," the glorified Lord
who is present in the eucharistic gifts. For in
the Eucharist, which is the moment of supreme
tension in the Church's mystical life, the great
atonement is lived in its full reality—that recon-
ciliation of the near and far, of the heavenly and
earthly. In the words of Paul : " He is our peace,
who hath made both one, and hath broken down the
middle wall of partition between us " . . . ; " For
it pleased the Father . . . that in Him should all
fulness dwell ; and, having made peace through the
blood of His Cross, by Him to reconcile all things
unto Himself ; by Him, I say, whether they be
things in earth, or things in heaven." [410]

CONCLUSION

For Christian Mysticism the glorification of the world is inseparably bound up with the incarnation, crucifixion and resurrection of the Son of God. Indeed, it is precisely through His death, Passion and humiliation that the victory over death and the glorification of life have been accomplished ! Here we have the deepest foundation of all Christianity, the essence of Paul's preaching, the inmost meaning of the liturgies, the " philosophy " of the Fathers. Athanasius, for instance, writes of the joy that has burst forth from His death : " Yea, verily, it is a thing rich in joy, this triumphant victory over death, and our incorruptibility (won) through that body of the Lord." [411] " God united Himself with our nature," says Gregory of Nyssa, " that our nature by union with God may become divine, as loosed from death and freed from subservience to the enemy ; for His resurrection from the dead is for mortal mankind a beginning of the resurrection unto eternal life." [412] " Thou hast united, O Lord," says the Syrian Liturgy of St James, " Thy divinity with our humanity and our humanity with Thy divinity, Thy life with our mortality and our mortality with Thy life ; Thou hast received what was ours and hast given unto us what was Thine, for the life and salvation of our souls, praise be to Thee in eternity." [413]

148

CONCLUSION

The coming consummation, the completed glorification, is still far off. "We groan, earnestly desiring to be clothed upon with our house which is from heaven," "waiting for the adoption, to wit, the redemption of our body." And the whole creation also "groaneth and travaileth in pain together until now." [414] Hence that eschatological spirit, that discontent with the earthly, that yearning of the soul towards the glorified future which is inseparably linked with Christianity. But the germ of immortality has already entered into the world and into life, and the faithful already know that "this corruptible must put on incorruption, and this mortal must put on immortality," already they know that "death is swallowed up in victory." [415] The whole message of primitive Christianity is concentrated in the words : "Christ is risen, the firstfruits of them that slept." And this pervades its whole philosophy, its whole apprehension of life, its whole faith. This is why the whole psychology of primitive Christianity, as we have seen, is so flooded with joy. In the same way the inmost and deepest life of Eastern Christianity finds its truest expression in the jubilant Easter cry : "Christ is risen." "Passover, Passover of the Lord : For from death to life and from earth to heaven hath Christ led us who sing the song of triumph." [416]

And already, now, in these earthly surroundings, Christianity has from the earliest times regarded the Sacrament of the body and blood of its Lord as a living pledge of the coming revelation of eternal life. And at the same time it regards this Lord's Supper as the highest expression of the continuing presence of the Lord among His people, as an act of union of the earthly with the heavenly, of the divine with the human,[417] whereby, already now, both the world and life are glorified in expectation of the final glorification to come. " Ye proclaim the Lord's death until He come " (R.V.), writes Paul to the Corinthians.[418] " May grace come and this world pass away ! " cries the oldest eucharistic prayer that has come down to us.[419] But once " He left in our hands the pledge of His sacred body, to be near us through His body and in all times to unite Himself with us through His power " (from a fragment of an ancient Eastern high prayer).[420]

And filled with the joyous consciousness of this divine presence, this faith gathers together all creation in one great family, one great organism, at the moment when the sacrifice of Golgotha is re-enacted for the faithful : " Thine from Thine we offer to Thee, for all men and for all things." [421]

NOTES

[1] I John i, 2 ; I Cor. xv, 14, 20.
[2] I John v, 4 ; I Thess. v, 16-18.
[3] Acts ii, 24, 32 ; iv, 2 ; iv, 53 ; x, 40-41, etc.
[4] I Cor. xv, 11.
[5] John iii, 15-16 ; iv, 14-17 ; vi, 33 et seq. ; v, 25 ; xi, 25 ; Rev. i, 17-18 ; ii, 10 ; I Cor. xv, 42 et seq. Cf. also John vii, 38 ; x, 10, 28 ; xii, 25 ; xiv, 6 ; xvii, 2-3 ; I John i, 1-2 ; ii, 25 ; v, 11 ; I Peter i, 3 ; Rom. viii, 11 ; x, 9 ; I Cor. vi, 14 ; 2 Cor. iv, 4 ; Phil. iii, 11, 21 ; 2 Tim. i, 10 ; Heb. ii, 14.
[6] For a good collection of Catacomb inscriptions, vide, e.g., " Monumenta ecclesiae liturgica," ed. Cabrol and Leclercq. Vol. I ; Reliquiae liturgicae vetustissimae, Sectio prima, 1902, p. ci et seq.
[7] Ad Rom., c. vi.
[8] Martyrium Polycarpi, c. xiv.
[9] " Didache," c. x. Cf. also the eucharistic prayer of the " Acts of John " (middle second century) : " . . . We praise Thy resurrection, which is manifested unto us through Thee. For Thou alone, O Lord, art the root of immortality and the source of incorruptibility " (σὺ γαρ εἶ μόνος, κύριε, ἡ ῥίζα τῆς ἀθανασιας και πηγη τῆς αφθαρσιας . . . c. 109). Also in an early Christian grace in chap. xii of the work, formerly attributed to Athanasius, " Of virginity," we read : " εὐχαριστοῦμεν σοι, πάτερ ἡμων, ὑπερ τῆς ἀγίας ἀναστασεως σοῦ : διὰ γὰρ Ἰησοῦ τοῦ παιδός σου ἐγνώρισας ἡμιν αὐτήν."
[10] Oden Salomos (Flemming's translation, 1910), xlii, 5, 6, 14-19, 25, 26.
[11] XI, 7-8.
[12] XV, 8.
[13] XI, 7-10.
[14] VI, 17.
[15] Cf. also the second letter of Clement (20, 5) : τῷ ἐξαποστείλαντι ἡμῖν τὸν σωτῆρα καὶ αρχηγὸν τῆς αφθαρσίας, δἰ οὗ και ἐφανέρωσεν ἡμῖν τὴν ἐπουράνιον ζωήν. Also in Ignatius, Eph. xvii, 1 : ἵνα πνέῃ τῃ ἐκκλησίᾳ ἀφθαρσιαν . . . ; ibid., xix, 3 : ἄγνοια καθῃρεῖτο, παλαιὰ βασιλεία διεφθείρατο θεοῦ ἀνθρωπίνως φανερομένου . . ., ἔνθεν τὰ πάντα συνεκινεῖτο διὰ τὸ μελετᾶσθαι θανάτου κατάλυσιν. Trall, ii, 1 : οὐ κατα ἄνθρωπον ζῶντες ἀλλὰ κατὰ Ἰησοῦν Χρ. τὸν δὲ ἡμᾶς ἀποθανόντα, ἵνα πιστεύσαντες εἰς τον θάνατου αὐτοῦ τὸ ἀποθανεῖν εκφύγητε. Eph. iii, 2 : I, Χρ. τὸ ἀδιάκριτον ἡμῶν ζῆν. Magn., I, 2 : . . . Ἰησοῦ Χριστοῦ τοῦ διὰ παντὸς ἡμας ζῆν. . . . Cf. Barnab., v, 6 (cf. R. Seeberg, Lehrbuch d. Dogmengesch., 1^3, 1922, pp. 145-148).
[16] I Cor. xv, 20, 22.

NOTES

[17] 2 Peter iii, 13 ; Rev. xxi, 1-4 ; Rom. viii, 21-22 ; 1 Cor. xv, 28. Cf. Rev. xxi, 5 ; xx, 14, and Acts iii, 21.

[18] " Gespräche Jesu mit seinen Jüngern." . . . Ed. Carl Schmidt, chap. ii.

[19] Chap. xii, p. 42.

[20] Chap. xxi, p. 72.

[21] Chap. xxv-xxvi, p. 82.

[22] Adv. haeres, iv, 18, 5.

[23] Epideix., 38, 39.

[24] *Vide* R. Seeberg, I, c. 410. The most important passages are quoted here, *e.g.*, Adv. haeres, iii, 18, 7 ; 23, 7 : "illius enim salus evacuatio est mortis ; domino igitur vivificante hominem id est Adam, evacuata est et mors." III, 19, 1 : "ignorantes autem eum, qui ex virgine est Emmanuel, privantur munere eius, quod est vita aeterna ; non recipientes autem verbum incorruptionis perseverant in carne mortali et sunt debitores mortis, antidotum mortis non accipientes." IV, 38, 4 : "Opportuerat autem primo naturam apparere, post deinde vinci et absorberi mortale ab immortalitate et corruptibile ab incorruptibilitate." V, 12, 6 : "et in semel totum sanum et integrum redintegravit hominem perfectum eum sibi praeparans ad resurrectionem " . . . etc.

[25] "Igitur, ut retexam : quam Deus manibus suis ad imaginem Dei struxit, quam de suo adflatu ad similitudinem suae vivacitatis animavit, quam incolatui, fructui, dominatui totius suae operationis praeposuit, quam sacramentis suis disciplinisque vestivit ; cujus munditias amat, cujus castigationes probat, cujus passiones sibi adpretiat—haeccine non resurget totiens Dei ? Absit, absit, ut Deus manum suarum operam, ingenii sui curam, adflatus sui vaginam, molitionis suae reginam, liberalitatis suae haeredem, religionis suae sacerdotem, testimonii sui militem, Christi sui sororem, in aeternum destituat interitum " . . . (c. ix). Also cc. viii, vii.

[26] De incarnatione Verbi, c. 54. Αὐτὸς ἐνηνθρώπησεν ἵνα ἡμεῖς θεοποιηθῶμεν, καὶ αὐτὸς ἐφανέρωσεν ἑαυτὸν δια σώματος, ἵνα ἡμεῖς τοῦ, ἀοράτου, πατρὸς ἔννοιαν λάβωμεν, καὶ αὐτὸς ὑπέμεινεν τὴν παρα ἀνθρώπου ὕβριν, ἵνα ἡμεῖς ἀθάνασίαν κληρονομήσωμεν. Cf. contra Arianos, i, 38, 39 ; ii, 47, 50 ; iii, 34. Ad Serap, i, 9, 24, etc. *Vide* "The Teaching of Athanasius concerning Deification," R. Seeberg, 113, 1923, pp. 80-82 ; K. Bornhaüser, " Die Vergottungslehre des Athanasius und Johannes Damascenus," 1903.

[27] Athanasius, Epistolae heortasticae, xi. Migne, t. 26, col. 1411 ; *vide* also especially epist. x (col. 1402).

[28] *Ibid.*, epist. vi (col. 1388).

[29] Cf. in particular epist. iii.

[30] De incarnatione Verbi, c. 9, 10, 13, 16, 20, 21, 24. Cf. κατάργησις τοῦ θανάτου (Arianos, I, 45), χατάκυσις θανάτου (ad Adelph., 5), et passim.

[31] *Ibid.*, c. 10. Cf. c. 27 : "That death is destroyed and the cross its victor, and that it is henceforth powerless, but in reality dead. For this there is no small proof and an open confirmation in that death is scorned by all the disciples of Christ, and they all mock death and no longer fear it, but in the sign of the cross and in faith in Christ tread it underfoot as a dead thing. For formerly, before

the divine coming of the Saviour, death was feared even by the holy, and all mourned the dead as those who had come to ruin. But now, after the Saviour has raised the body, death has lost its terror, and all who believe on Christ tread it underfoot, as though it were nothing." . . . Cf. also the splendid dying prayer of the sister of Gregory of Nyssa, Makrina : " Thou, Lord, hast destroyed in us the fear of death, Thou hast made the end of this earthly life the beginning of the heavenly ! Thou dost let our bodies rest for a time in sleep and dost awaken them again out of sleep with the last trumpet ! Thou dost give the earth, which Thou hast made with Thine hands, for the raising of the earth and takest again what Thou hast given, and changest into incorruptibility and beauty what is mortal and ugly ! . . . Thou hast opened unto us the way of the resurrection by breaking down the gates of Hades, and hast destroyed that which had the power of death " (cf. Harnack, Dogmengesch, 114, 1909, p. 60). Cf. also, *e.g.*, Athanasius contra Arianos, or. ii, 61.

[32] Greg. Nyss. Catech. magn., c. 25.

[33] Joannis Chrysostomi, De resurrect. mort., cap. 6 ; cf. cap. 7.

[34] *Ibid.*, In Epist. i ad Cor. Homil. xxix, 2.

[35] *Ibid.*, in Epist. ad Rom. Homil. xiv.

[36] S. Ephraemi Syri. Carmina Nisibena, ed. G. Bickell, 1866 (xlvii).

[37] Carmen, lxix.

[38] Carmen, xliii. Cf. also xliv, xlv, xlvi, xlviii, lxv.

[39] Cf. also Athanasius (see above).

[40] Cf. Oktoichos . . . The Orthodox Catholic Church of the East, ed. Probst A. v. Maltzew, 1903, part i, pp. 634-635. Part ii, 5, 1103 ; i. 1254.

[41] Oktoichos, i, 332, 924, 1253.

[42] This appears with particular emphasis in the " Kanones Stauroanastasimoi " (the " Cross- Resurrection "-songs).

[43] Oktoichos, i, 42, 974, 43-44, 1003.

[44] I, 57, 689, 694, 688, 699.

[45] Oktoichos, i, 71.

[46] *Ibid.*, i, 73, 17 ; ii, 339 (cf. ii, 65, 366), 885 ; i, 26 (cf. ii. 10) ; i, 693.

[47] I, 15.

[48] II, 357.

[49] I, 684.

[50] II, 616.

[51] II, 885.

[52] Printed in the Russian paper of Helsingfors, *Russkia Westi*, 6th Sept. 1922 (No. 66).

[53] See the collection of materials on the persecution of the Church and religion by the Bolsheviks : " The Assault of Heaven," London, 1924.

[54] And it rings out again in this wonderful poem of contrition of the Eastern Church :

" I have sinned above all other men, I alone have sinned against Thee. But have mercy, O Saviour, as God on Thy creature."

" I have made unclean the garment of my flesh and have defiled, O Saviour, that which in me was made after Thy form and image."

NOTES

" I have darkened the beauty of my soul through the lusts of my passions and brought my whole understanding to dust."

" I rent my first garment that the Creator had woven for me from the beginning, and therefore I lie naked."

" I put on a torn garment, that the serpent wove for me, and now I am ashamed." . . .

" I alone have sinned against Thee, I have sinned above all others. O Christ, Saviour, forsake me not."

" Thou art the Good Shepherd, seek me, Thy lamb ; though I have strayed, forsake me not." . . .

" O supreme Trinity, that art worshipped in unity, take away from me the burden of my sins, which are heavy, and in mercy give me tears of repentance " . . ., etc.

[55] *Vide, e.g.*, Nicephoros the Anchorite : " Sobriety and the keeping of the Heart " (" Dobrotolubie," Band v, pp. 264-265).

[56] Macar. Aeg., " Liber de elevatione mentis," c. 20 (Migne, i, 34, col. 900).

[57] Thus, *e.g.*, John Climax, Nicephoros the Anchorite (" Dobrotolubie," v, 266).

[58] Dobrotolubie, ii, 166-167.

[59] In this connection Hesychius of Jerusalem says, for instance : " Spiritual restraint is the way of all virtue and of the commandments of God. It is also called stillness of the heart and it is the same as defence of the soul which is kept free from all vain imaginings " (Dobrot., ii, 166).

[60] Dobrotol., v, 252-253.

[61] Hesychius of Jerusalem (Dobrotol., ii, 170).

[62] Migne, t. 34, col. 633, 907, 623.

[63] Dobrotol., ii, 173.

[64] Apophtegmata Patrum (Migne, Patr. Gr., i, 65, col. 396).

[65] Isaac the Syrian, Homily, 48 (Russian edition, 1911). Cf. the English translation. *Mystic Treatises by Isaac of Nineveh*, transl. from Bedian's Syriac text by A. J. Wensinck, Amsterdam, 1923.

[66] Isaac the Syrian (Dobrotol., ii, 730-731 ; cf. p. 737).

[67] Dobrotol., ii, 648.

[68] Cf. what is said on this point by the great Russian thinker and theologian, A. Chomiakov, in his remarkable Monograph on the Church (published posthumously in his " Works "—in Russian, vol. ii, 1867, p. 22). Cf. also the work of the great Russian expounder of the ascetic life—Bishop Theophanus (middle of nineteenth century), also the book of Professor Sarin, " Asceticism " (Russian), vol. i, 1906.

[69] Dobrotolubie, iii, 557.

[70] *Vide* Euagrius Ponticus, Capita practica ad Anatolium, 92 (Migne, vol. 40, col. 1249).

[71] Isaac the Syrian, 48. Sermon.

[72] Apophtegmata Patrum (Migne, Patr. Graes., vol. 65, col. 379-381). These words are attributed to Paul the Hermit. Similar words are written in connection with Saint Sergius of Radonesch by his biographer Epiphanius.

NOTES

[73] *Otkrovennye raskasy strannika . . .*, p. 31. Cf. pp. 39-40, 93. There is now a German translation of this wonderful little book : *Ein Russisches Pilgerleben* hrsggb. von Reinhold von Walter, Berlin, 1925.

[74] This cry which occurs already in the Clementine Liturgy is a regular feature of the Eastern Mass.

[75] From the Byzantine Liturgy of the pre-sanctified gifts (in place of the Song of the Cherubim).

[76] Sung in St Basil's Liturgy for Easter Saturday (taken from the old Greek Liturgy of St James).

[77] And so in a number of liturgies of the Eastern Church, *e.g.*, the Syrian Liturgy of St James (Renaudot's Liturgiarum Orientalium Collectio, 1847, ii, 38, 40. Cf. 32, 30, 136, etc.). Cf. also in many places in the writings of the Fathers of the Church, Chrysostom, " De Penitentia," Hom. ix (Migne, 49, col. 345), etc.

[78] The second prayer before the Communion (St John Chrysostom).

[79] The second prayer before the Communion (*ibid.*).

[80] *Vide* generally the prayers before the Communion of the Eastern Church.

[81] German translation, pub. Maltzew, Liturgikon, 1902, p. 215.

[82] " Canon " before the Communion, canto 8.

[83] Brightman, " Liturgies Eastern and Western," 1896, i, 132, 176 ; cf. Renaudot's Liturgiarum Orientalium Collectio, i, 45.

[84] For this eschatological aspect of the celebration of the Lord's Supper and regarding the Eucharist in general, *vide*, *e.g.*, my essay, " Glorification of the World in the Eucharist," forming the last chapter of my work : " Glorification of the World and of life in Mysticism."

[85] A. Chomiakov, " Collected Works " (Russian), vol. ii, 1867, pp. 18-20.

[86] *Vide* in this connection the splendid passages in A. Chomiakov's " A few words by an Orthodox Christian " (1853), " Collected Works," vol. ii, 1867, p. 49 (German translation in the collection " Östliches Christentum," pub. H. Ehrenberg, vol. i, 1923, p. 162).

[87] Easter Greeting of the Eastern Church.

[88] Cf. my essay : " Archiv f. Religionswissenschaft," 1923, H. 3-4.

[89] Cf., *e.g.*, Plot. Ennead., vi, 7, 39.

[90] Santa Teresa, Escritos, tomo primero (Biblioteca de autores espanoles, 53), Madrid, 1861, p. 511 (Poesia, v).

[91] Cf. Augustine *Confessions*, x, 27.

[92] John iii, 29.

[93] Cf., for instance, this cry of a contemporary mystic : " Je me suis penchée sur la source vive et j'ai été désaltérée " (Th. Flournoy, " Une mystique moderne " in " Archives de Psychologie," xv, 1915, p. 103).

[94] 1 John i, 2 ; John i, 16.

[95] Matt. xiii, 44-46, 49.

[96] Ephesians iii, 8.

[97] Colossians i, 27.

[98] 2 Cor. iv, 6-7, etc.

[99] Ephesians v, 19-20.

NOTES

[100] 1 Thess. v, 16-18 ; 2 Cor. vi, 10 ; vii, 4 ; cf. Phil. iv, 7 ; iii, 1 ; 2 Cor. iii, 11 *et seq.*, etc.

[101] Epistle of Barnabas, vii, 1 ; cf. Hermae Pastor Mandat, xi, 2. *The Odes of Solomon*, 7, 8, 15, 40, 41, etc.

[102] Cf. Martyrium Polycarpi : "θάρσους καὶ χαρὰς ἐνεπίμπλατο καὶ τὸ πρῶσοπον αὐτοῦ χάριτος ἐπληροῦτο" (c. xii, cf. c. xiv), Acts of Carpus, 38-39 (". . . εἶδον τὴν δόξαν κυρίου καὶ ἐχάρην" . . .), 41 ; of the Lugdunian Martyrs we read : "ἐκείνους μὲν ἐπεκούφιζεν ἡ χαρὰ τῆς μαρτυρίας" . . . "οἱ μὲν γὰρ ἱλαροὶ προῄεσαν, δόξης καὶ χάριτος πολλῆς ταῖς ὄψεσιν αὐτῶν συγκεκραμένης" (34, 35). Cf. Martyrium der Perpetua und Felicitas, c. xviii, etc.

[103] John xv, 11 ; cf. xvi, 20, 22, 24.

[104] Palladius Historia Lausaica, c. 97.

[105] Philokalia (the great mystico-ascetic chrestomathy of the Christian East), vol. ii (Russian edition, 1889), p. 722.

[106] *Ibid.*, vol. iii, p. 401.

[107] "Tanto repletus est gaudio, quod non capiens se pro laetitia, etiam nolens de hujus modi secretis in aures aliquid hominum eructabat". La Leggenda di San Francesco scritta da tre suoi compagni (legenda trium sociorum), Rome, 1899, c. 5.

[108] ". . . coepit per plateas et vicos civitatis, tamquam ebrius spiritu, dominum collaudare," *ibid.*, c. 7.

[109] *Ibid.*, c. ii.

[110] Jacopone da Todi, Laude, xxvi, xxxi (edition of his "Laude" in the series "Scritori d'Italia," 1915).

[111] Cf., for instance, "Aufzeichnungen über das mystische Leben der Nonnen von Kirchberg" (Alemania, xxi, 1893), pp. 105, 107, 110, 111, 113 ; also H. Wilms : "Das Beten der Mystikerinnen," published from the Chronicles of the Dominican Convents, 1916, p. 173.

[112] Also : "But this is only an example, or glimpse of the Son of God in men, whereby the faith is strengthened and maintained ; for joy cannot be as great in an earthly vessel as in a heavenly where the power of God is complete" (Aurora, iii, 15-17). For the joy of the soul penetrated by the Holy Spirit, *vide* also, *e.g.*, i, 102. For joy in the Divinity Himself, *vide* also, *e.g.*, iii, 11, 20-24 ; xii, 23 *et seq.* : "De signatura rerum," xvi, 2 *passim*.

[113] Streeter and Appasamy, "The Sadhu : A Study in Mysticism and Practical Religion," London, 1921. Cf. Heiler, Sadhu Sundar Singh, 1924, 83 *et seq.*

[114] "Otkrovennye raskazy strannika duchovnomu otzu swoemu," Kazan, 3rd edition, 1884, p. 59 ; cf. pp. 19-20, 36, 40.

[115] Dhammapadam, 200.

[116] Suttai Nipáta, 813, 33.

[117] Chándogya-Up., 4, 9, 2 ; cf. Mahávagga, i, 23, 6, 23, 4 (Sacred books of the East, xiii, pp. 147, 145) ; Majjh-Nik., 185.

[118] Kath-Up., 5, 14 ; cf. 5, 12. Also cf. Svetásvat. Up., 4, 18 ; Kath-Up., 2, 12-13 ; Maitr. Up., vi, 30 ; vi, 34, 4 ; vi, 34, 9.

[119] Taittiriya-Up., 3, 6 ; cf. Maitr. Up., 4, 4.

[120] Bhagavadgitâ, x, 9 ; cf. vi, 21, 27, 28.

[121] *E.g.*, vii, 18, 19.

NOTES

[122] G. U. Pope, Tiruváçagam or the Sacred Utterances of Mânikka Vâçagar, 1900, hymn xxxvii, 6, 9.

[123] One hundred poems of Kabir, translated by Rabindranath Tagore, hymn xvii (cf. also the state of spiritual joy as it is described in the "Psalms of Maratha Saints," translated by Nic. Macnicol, 1919). Cf. also similar accounts by the Indian poet and mystic Tukaram (seventeenth century A.D., quoted in Sydney Cave, Redemption, Hindu and Christian, 1919, p. 118). In Julal eddin Rumi God says : "Except My service, which is joy's sunrise, Man has never felt and never will feel an impression of joy ! "—Selected poems from the Divini Shamsi Tabriz, trans. by Reynolds A. Nicholson, 1898, p. 179.

[124] 2 Cor. v, 17.

[125] Juan de la Cruz, Cántico espiritual.

[126] Cf., e.g., Underhill, "Mysticism," 1911, pp. 304-313.

[127] George Fox, "Journal," p. 17, London, J. M. Dent & Sons, Ltd.

[128] Jacob Boehme, "Aurora," xix, 11-13.

[129] Or. 26 quoted in Holl, Enthusiasmus u. Bussgewalt beim griech Mönchtum, 1898, p. 81 (cf. Migne, Patr. Gr., t. 120, col. 449CD). The nature of things changes according to the inward state of "the soul" (first hundred chapters on the "Active Life," "Philokalia," Russian edition, second ed., Moscow, 1900, vol. v, p. 95).

[130] Ven. Catharinae de Geweswiler, "De vitis primarum sororum monasterii (in J. Pez, Bibliotheca ascetia, viii, Ratisbona, 1725, p. 124).

[131] Beatae Angelae de Fulginio, Visionum et instructionum liber, Colonia, 1851 (Bibliotheca mystica et ascetica), c. xx, p. 66.

[132] Ibid., c. xxii : "et statim fuerunt aperti oculi animae meae et videbam unam plenitudinem Dei, in qua comprehendebam totum mundum et mare et abyssum et omnia, in quibus non videbam nisi tantum potentiam divinam, modo omnino inenarrabili. Et anima admirando exclamavit dicens : Est iste mundus plenus de Deo ! Et comprehendebam totum mundum quasi quid parum. Et videbam potentiam Dei excedere omnia et implere omnia." Cf. also c. xxix— God speaks to the soul : ". . . Scias, quod totus mundus est plenus de me. Et tunc videbam, quod omnis creatura erat plena ipso."

[133] One hundred poems of Kabir . . ., lxxvi, xli, i ; cf. vii, xvi, xiv, xviii, xcvii.

[134] G. M. Pope, The Tiruváçagam, hymn xxxvii, 8 ; cf. v, 48, 70 ; cf., e.g., also "Psalms of Maratha Saints," translated by Nicol Macnicol, 1919, No. xii (a hymn of Tukaram).

[135] Quoted in Sir R. J. Bhandarkar, Vaisnavism, Saivism . . ., 1913, p. 95. Cf. also the following words in Saint Theresa : "I understood how God is present in all things and the image of a sponge filled with water appeared to my soul" (Relacion, ix, 10, quoted in Underhill, l.c.). I should like to quote here just one more example from Persian mysticism, the passage from Farid-eddin-Attar's "Talk of the Birds," in which the glorification of the world is described with all the glow of Oriental colouring. For whosoever has reached the stage of knowledge, "the glowing oven of the world

NOTES

is transformed into a garden of delight. He then beholds the almond in its shell " (*i.e.*, God in all things), " or rather sees nothing except the object of his love. In everything on which his eye falls, he sees His face. . . . Through this veil, shining like the sun, countless mysteries are revealed to his sight " (Third Valley, translated in Silvestre de Sacy's Pend-Nameh ou le livre des conseils de Ferideddin-Attar, 1819, p. 177).

[136] Quoted in Reynolds A. Nicholson's " The Mystics of Islam," 1914, p. 59. Cf. the mystic experience of Sister Anna von Selen of the Convent of Adelhausen (in Southern Baden) at the end of the thirteenth century : " Zu einemmale da kam si in söliche einberunge mit Gotte an irme gebette, das ir Gotte als luterlich erschien, da si darnach wz fünff wochen, was si sach das wand si, es were Gott " . . . (Die Chronik der Anna von Munzingen, herausg. von Prof. J. König, Freiburg Diöcesan-Archiv, Bd. xiii, 1880, p. 154).

[137] In Reynolds A. Nicholson's " Studies in Islamic Mysticism," 1921, p. 235.

[138] Selected poems from the Divini Shamsi Tabriz, edited and translated by Reynolds A. Nicholson, 1898, No. ix (p. 33). A similar feeling of the overwhelming power of the love which inundates the whole world, embracing us from every side and penetrating the soul through the medium of all our senses, nay, " besieging " it and driving it into a corner, appears also in the Renaissance philosopher, Giordano Bruno (" Degli eroici furori," Son., No. 51), and in the work of Francis's ardent disciple, the poet and mystic, Jacopone da Todi (Lauda, lxxxii).

[139] The pantheistic note is very marked and definite in the Sufis, and appears with special force, for instance, in the poem of Ibnu'l Farid (*vide* R. A. Nicholson's " Studies in Islamic Mysticism," 1921). Religious experience also bears a definitely pantheistic colouring in Manikka Vasagar (*vide* G. M. Pope's " The Tiruváçagam," *e.g.*, hymn v, 70, p. 72) and in Tukaram (*vide, e.g.*, Sir R. G. Bhandarkar, l.c., 97 ; cf. also " Psalms of Maratha Saints," translated by N. Macnicol, p. 21). *Vide* also Hymn xiv in " One Hundred Poems of Kabir."

[140] Cf., *e.g.*, N. Macnicol, l.c., p. 28.

[141] *Vide, e.g.*, R. A. Nicholson's " Studies in Islamic Mysticism," p. 131 ; also the same author's " The Idea of Personality in Sufism," 1923, p. 51 (passages from Jili and Jalâl eddîn Rumî).

[142] 1 John v, 19 ; John xvi, 33 ; Romans vii, 24.

[143] John i, 14.

[144] Isaiah liii, 4.

[145] Gal. ii, 20 ; 2 Cor. i, 5 ; vii, 4 ; Col. i, 24.

[146] Luke xvii, 21.

[147] Matt. xxviii, 20.

[148] John xv, 4.

[149] Col. i, 27 ; iii, 4 ; Phil. i, 21.

[150] Rom. xiv, 7-9 ; vi, 4.

[151] 1 Cor. vi, 19-20 ; cf. iii, 16.

[152] 1 Cor. xv, 54.

[153] John i, 14.

NOTES

[154] John xvi, 33.

[155] 1 John i, 1-2 ; cf., *e.g.*, The Message of the Risen Lord in Acts.

[156] 1 Cor. xv, 20, 26.

[157] Theaet., 176A.

[158] " . . . existente providentia, mala quoque necessaria substitisse. Propterea quod silva sit et eadem sit malitia praedita. . . . Proptereaque Numenius laudat Heraclitum, reprehendentem Homerum, qui optaverit interitum ac vestitatem malis vitae, quod non intelligeret mundum sibi deleri placere, si quidem silva, quae malorum fons est, exterminaretur " (also xvi ; cf. also xviii ; Numenios of Apamea, the Father of Neo-Platonism. Works. Biography by Kenneth Guthrie, 1917, pp. 10-13, 16-17).

[159] *E.g.*, Enn., i, 1, 8, c. 7 ; i, 2, c. 2. Enn., iii, 1, 3, c. 7 *passim*; Maximus Tyrius, xli.

[160] Tim. 48A, 68E ; also, *e.g.*, Maximus Tyrius, xli, and Numenios, also xv-xviii ; Enn. i, 1, 8, c. 7.

[161] Enn., i, i, 1, c. 8, c. 3, 3-5, 7, 8, 14 ; cf. Numenios, xvi, xvii.

[162] Cf., *e.g.*, the famous Mythos in Plato's " Politicus," 269D-273E, etc.

[163] Inspired praise of the cosmos is also to be found in the " Timaeus " 28B, 37A, 68E, 92C, in the " Laws," x, 896 *et seq.*, in many parts of the Enneades (*e.g.*, ii, 1, 9, c. 5, 16-18 ; iii, 1, 2, c. 3, 13, 15, 17), also in the Platonistic tract of the first century A.D. " De mundo " (especially in chap. v), etc. And in Plato's " Supper," as is known, earthly beauty is apprehended as a preliminary step towards the perception of primitive beauty, as a reflection of this beauty and a reminder of it.

[164] Enn., vi, 1, 9, c. 11 ; Theaet., 176A ; cf. Enn., i, 1, 8, c. 7, 8 *passim*.

[165] Phaedo., 62B, 82E ; Cratylos, 400C ; Gorgias, 493A.

[166] *Ibid.*, 81A ; cf. in Plotinus : κακὸν δὲ ειναι τὴν τοιαύτην κοινωνίαν καὶ ἀγαθὸν τὴν ἀπαλλαγήν (Enn., vi, 4, 16).

[167] " The Republic," Book vii ; Enn., iv, 8, 3.

[168] This thought seems to have been expressed in similar form already by Plato : " Even if God could, He would not abolish evil " (translated from Theophrast., Metaph., pp. 322 *et seq.* Br.; quoted in E. Schröder's " Plotinos Abhandlung," πόθεν τὰ κακά, 1916, p. 30).

[169] Enn., iii, 1, 3, c. 3 ; i, 2, c. 11, 17, 5 ; cf. also c. 2, 3, 4.

[170] Cf., *e.g.*, Celsus (in Origenes contra Celsum, iv, 69 ; Maximus Tyrius, 41).

[171] Cf. " Symposium," 207-208B. Regarding the dominion of death, *vide* also Phaedo., p. 110 (ed. Astius). Heraklitos had already said : θάνατός ἐστιν ὁκόσα ἐγερθέντες ὀρέομεν (ap. Clem. Alex. Strom., iii, 3, p. 520, 7).

[172] Ap. Origen. contra Celsum, iv, c. 65. The idea of the eternal cyclic return of all existing things was widespread in antiquity. We encounter it in Plato and Aristotle ; in later times it is become a commonplace of philosophy. For fuller treatment *vide* Hans Meyer's " Zur Lehre von der ewigen Wiederkunft aller Dinge " (Beiträge zur Gesch. des christl. Altertums. Festgabe Albert Ehrhard, 1922, pp. 363 *et seq.*).

NOTES

[173] Cf., *e.g.*, Maximus Tyrius, xi, 4, 5.

[174] The Stoics tell us that evil is indispensable to this harmony of the whole. Chrysippus maintains that " It is impossible to abolish evil, but it would not be desirable to abolish it," Arnim, Stoicorum veterum fragmenta, ii, fr. 1182 ; cf. 1181 (1169). The mutation, transience and destruction of every single thing and individual is the condition of this general harmony and of the constant self-renewal of the cosmos (*vide, e.g.*, Marcus Aurel., vii, 18, 19, 23, 25 ; viii, 18, 20, etc.). The laws of the fate that rules the world are inflexible and unalterable. This even the gods cannot alter, it is the " eternal truth " (veritas sempiterna), " The eternal cause of things " (causa aeterna rerum) (Arnim, ii, fr. 921, 923, 924). One thing lives at the cost and through the death of another, and everything returns in fixed cycles, and there is nothing new under the sun ! (*ibid.*, i, fr. 109 ; ii, fr. 623. M. Aurel., ii, 14 ; vi, 46 ; vii, 49 ; viii, 6). Regarding the cosmic idea—the justification of the world and of the evil in the world, *vide* also the masterly exposition by E. Schröder of the treatise of Plotinus, ποθέν τα κακά (Enn., i, 8), Rostocker Diss., 1916, p. 40 *et seq.*

[175] *Vide, e.g.*, Arnim, i, c. 1, fr. 98 ; iii, 172, 537 ; ii, 937, 1131 ; also in Marc. Aurel., ii, 3 ; iv, 23 ; v, 8 ; vi, 1, 36 ; vii, 9 ; in Epictetus also, *e.g.*, the stoically coloured hymn to Nature in the collection of Orphean Hymns (x), etc.

[176] *E.g.*, ii, 2, 11, 17 ; iv, 15 ; vi, 56, 59 ; vii, 1, 6, 10, 21, 49, 50 ; viii, 5, 21, etc.

[177] VI, 46.

[178] Rom. viii, 21-23 ; 1 Cor. xv, 28 ; Rev. xxi, 5 ; cf. xxi, 1-7 ; xx, 14. Cf. 2 Peter iii, 13 : " We, according to His promise, look for new heavens and a new earth, wherein dwelleth righteousness." Cf. Acts iii, 21.

[179] Isa. lxv, xvii, lxvi, xxii. Cf. also Isa. ii.

[180] 91, 16-17 (in the translation of R. H. Charles, The Book of Enoch or 1 Enoch, 1912, pp. 233-234). Cf. 72, 1 : The angel Uriel shows to Enoch the laws of the star world, which retain their power until a new creation is accomplished, lasting unto eternity. Cf. also the " picture speeches " chap. of the Book of Enoch to which, incidentally, some scholars have ascribed a much later, post-Christian date, though it is generally placed in the first century B.C. Here, too, mention is made of a " new Heaven " and a " new earth " (chap. 45, 4-5 : " I will change the heaven and make of it an eternal blessing and light. And I will change the earth and make it a blessing "), and also of " eternal life " (chap. 37, 4 ; 40, 9 ; and especially chap. 58) : " The chosen shall be in the light of eternal life . . . and there shall be a light to which there is no end," verses 3, 6.

[181] Dan. xii, 2. A sketch of these expectations of later Judaism is to be found, *e.g.*, in Volz's " Die Judische Eschatologie von Daniel bis Akiba," 1903 ; J. Lindblom's " Das Ewige Leben." A study of the origin of the religious idea of life in the New Testament, Upsala, 1914, pp. 33 *et seq.*, 48 *et seq.* (a rich collection of texts), Ed. Meyer's " Ursprung und Anfänge des Christentums," 2 vols., 1921, pp. 174 *et seq.*, R. H. Charles, " A Critical Commentary on the

Revelation of St John," 1920, vol. ii, pp. 20, 208, etc. These hopes appear with special intensity in some of the later Jewish literature (about the end of the first century A.D.) : in the Syrian Baruch Apocalypse (44, 11, 51, and also 21, 23 ; 32, 6), in the Book of Esdras (8, 53 *et seq.* ; 7, 13, 75), in the Slav Enoch (Destruction of time !—chap. 65, 6-7 ; cf. Rev. 10, 6).

[181a] 1 John v, 4.

[182] 1 Cor. xv, 57.

[183] Isaac the Syrian, 48. Sermon.

[184] Palladius, Historia Lausaica, c. 45 ; cf. Rufinus, Historia monachorum, c. 6.

[185] Johannes Moschus, Pratum spirituale, c. 2.

[186] Sulpicius Severus, Dialogus i (De virtutibus monachorum orientalium), c. 14. Cf. also, *e.g.*, the life of Saint Lukas, the Monk (a Greek saint of the tenth century) who fed birds and even snakes (Max Herzog von Sachsen, Das christliche Hellas, 1918, p. 118). Cf. also the life of the Abyssinian saint, Jafkeran-Egsie (*vide* Turajew, " Some Lives of Abyssinian Saints "—Vizantijskij Vremennik, vol. xiii, book 2, 1906 (Russian)).

[187] Cf., *e.g.*, Palladius, c. 19 ; Joh. Moschus, c. 18 ; Sulpicius Severus, c. 13-15, also, *e.g.*, the old life of Saint Sabbas. Cf. also the Russian Lives of the Saints.

[188] Apophtegmata patrum (Migne, Patr. Gr., 65, col. 379 to 381). Similar accounts are given of the submission of the wild animals to Saint Sergius of Radonesch by his biographer and disciple, Epiphanius.

[189] Sulp. Sev., c. 15.

[190] " Philokalia " (the famous and comprehensive ascetico-mystical chrestomathy of the Christian East), Russian ed., vol. ii, p. 557 ; Migne, Patr. Gr., i, 88, col. 892.

[191] Τὸ ἐμὸν βίβλιον ἡ φύσις τῶν γεγονότων ἐστὶ καὶ πάρεστιν, ὅτε βούλομαι τοὺς λόγους ἀναγίγνώσκειν τοῦ θεοῦ (*v.* Euagrius Ponticus (fourth century), Capita practica ad Anatolium, 92 ; Mi, t. 40, c. 1249).

[192] Caesarius Heisterbacensis, Dialogus miraculorum, Diet. xii, c. 4.

[193] *Ibid.*, iv, 17 : " De converso, qui voce cuculi deceptus in apostasia mortuus est." How totally different—illumined by joy—is this voice of the cuckoo calling in the spring felt by the great English poet Wordsworth :

> " O blithe new-comer ! I have heard,
> I hear thee and rejoice.
> O cuckoo ! shall I call thee bird,
> Or but a wandering voice ? " etc.

[194] *Vide* also Caes. Heist., l.c., iv, 5, 6, 7, 33, 35, 48 ; Catharinae de Geweswiler, De vitis primarum sororum monasterii sui (Pez, Bibl. ascetia, vol. viii, 1725), c. 13, 28.

[195] Caes. Heist., iv, 5 : " Statim affuit inimicus in forma lucidissime oculi habentis quantitatem pugni, in quo quicquid erat vivere putabatur."

NOTES

[196] *E.g.*, Exordium magnum ordinis Cisterciensis Dist., iv, c. 4 (Migne, Patr. lat., t. 185, col. 1099; Herberti, De miraculi, i, 19; Mi., 185, col. 1291, end of twelfth century); cf. also quotations below from the work of the Abbot Richalmus, also Agnetis Blannbekin (end of fourteenth century), Vita et Revelationes, c. 200.

[197] Richalmi Abbatis (about 1270), Liber Revelationum de insidiis et versutiis daemonum adversus homines (Pez, Thesaurus anecdotorum novissimus, t. i, par. 2), c. i, 3 *passim*.

[198] *Ibid.*, c. i; Agnetis Blannbekin, c. 66.

[199] *Vide, e.g.*, Petri Venerabilis (twelfth century), De miraculis, i, 14 (Migne, 189, col. 877); Richalmus, c. 15; Caesarius, c. 33.

[200] *E.g.*, Caes. Heist., iv, 28.

[201] There are a number of examples in A. Graf's " Geschichte des Teufels."

[202] Cf., *e.g.*, Caesarius, iv, 30, 31.

[203] Caes., iv, 54.

[204] Richalmus, l.c., especially chapters 28, 21, 22, 12, 37, etc.

[205] *Ibid.*, cap. (col. 385).

[206] *Ibid.*, c. 10 (col. 395).

[207] C. ii (col. 395).

[208] C. 12 (col. 396); c. 41 (col. 421).

[209] C. 22 (col. 410).

[210] *Vide, e.g.*, E. Male, " L'Art Religieux de la Fin du Moyen Age en France," 1908, pp. 371-422; Remy de Gourmont, " Le Latin Mystique," 1913, pp. 12 *et seq.*, 228-229; also Seelmann's " Die Totentänze des Mittelalters," 1893; A. Dürrwachter's " Die Totentanzforschung," 1914; Weber, F., " Aspects of Death in Art and Epigram," 1914; Stefan Glixelli's " Les Cinq Poèmes des trois Morts et des Trois Vifs," Paris, 1914, etc.

[211] " We believe that God is everywhere present, but we believe this beyond all doubt when we rise for divine service." Reg. S. Ben., 19.

[212] Caes. Heist., vii, 12; cf. the " Diessenhofensche Chronik," " Leben heiliger alemmanischer Frauen des Mittelalters, V. die Nonnen von Katainenthal bei Diessenhofen," ed. A. Birlinger (Alemania, xv, 1887), p. 159; also Elsbeth Stagel, "Leben der Schwestern zu Töss," ed. F. Vetter (Deutsche Texte des Mittelalters, Bd. vi, 1906), p. 21.

[213] Caes. Heist., vii, 47.

[214] *Ibid.*, vii, 13, 14; cf. Diessenhofen, p. 159.

[215] *Vide, e.g.*, a vision described in Ven. Joannis de Ellenbogen. . . . " De vita venerabilium monachorum monasterii sui liber " (beginning of fourteenth century): a monk once sees at night " gloriosam processionem albatorum de summo altari quasi per ambitum procedentem. Et ipsa, visione (durante) tabula pro mortuo percussa fuit, et Conventus in Infirmitorio unum Monachum, trahentem ultimum Spiritum, invenit. Et sic arbitror, animam ipsius Monachi albatos, id est Sanctos in ipsa hora, qua expiravit, in suum consortium feliciter assumpsisse." (In Pez, Bibliotheca ascetia, viii, 1725, v. 478-479.)

[216] Cf., *e.g.*, " Actus Beati Francisci et sociorum ejus " (ed. P.

NOTES

Sabatier, 1902), c. 52 ; Agnetis Blannbekin, Vita et Revelationes (ed. B. Pez, 1731), c. lxv ; also " Die Fragmente der Libri viii Miraculorum des Caesarius von Heisterbach," lib. i, c. 4 (ed. Dr Aloys Meister, Römische Quartalschrift, 1901) ; Catharinae de Geweswiler, l.c., xxxvi, etc., also a number of visions in the story of the Grail.

[217] Cf., e.g., Catharinae de Geweswiler, l.c., xxxvi, Visions in the story of the Grail, etc.

[218] A quantity of evidence is given in Wilms' " Das Beten der Mystikerinnen nach der Chroniken der Dominikanerinnen-Kloster," 1916, p. 161.

[219] Cf., e.g., The Visions of Catherine of Geneva (Vita e dottrina, c. ii, 6).

[220] Proofs are cited in my essay : " The Figure of the Suffering Christ in the Religious Experience of the Middle Ages " in " Trudy russkych učjonych sa granitsei," vol. ii, Berlin, 1923.

[221] Cf., e.g., Exordium magnum ordinis Cisterciensis, dist. iii, c. 16 (Mi., 185, col. 1074) ; Catharinae de Geweswiler, l.c., c. xxiv, pp. 199-200.

[222] A monk of the monastery of Clairvaux to whom Christ twice appeared feels thereafter the divine presence everywhere—" felici doctus experimento, credidit ubique divinam esse praesentiam " (Exordium magnum . . . Dist. iv, c. 8, Migne, t. 185, col. 1103). Cf. the words quoted from the monastery ordinances of St Benedictus !

[223] For the meekness of God, vide, e.g., Angelae de Fulginio, Revelationum et instructionum liber, c. xxii (Colonae, 1851, p. 79) : " Et dixit mihi : Vidisti aliquid de potentia mea, modo vide et humilitaten meam. Et videbam tantam profunditatem Dei ad homines et tantam humilitatem, quod comprehendens anima potentiam inenarrabilem et videns tam profundam humilitatem mirabatur." Cf. also the words of Francis of Assisi concerning the infinite meekness of God as they are quoted in the Sacrament of the Lord's Supper : " O humilitas sublimis ! O sublimitas humilis, quod Dominus universitatis, Deus et Dei filius sic se humiliat, et pro nostra salute sub modica panis formula se abscondat " (" Epistula ad Capitulum generale," 2, in Boehme's " Analecten zur Geschichte des Franziscus von Assisi," 1904, p. 59).

[224] Matt. xxv, 40, vide my work : " The Figure of the Suffering Christ," where further evidence is given.

[225] Vide, e.g., Yrjö Hirn, " The Sacred Shrine," London, 1912, ch. v, viii.

[226] " Ecce quotidie humiliat se, sicut quando a regalibus sedibus venit, in uterum Virginis, cotidie venit ad nos ipse humilis apparens, cotidie descendit de sinu Patris super altare in manibus sacerdotis," cries Francis of Assisi, for instance, in fear and trembling (" Verba Admonitionis," I, Boehme, l.c., p. 41).

[227] There are countless examples of this in the literature of the Middle Ages. Cf., e.g., many of the stories in Caesarius Heisterbach, and in his " Dialogus miraculorum," lib. i, and in the first and second books of his " Libri viii miraculorum," or, e.g., an old Italian work :

NOTES

"I miracoli del Santissimo sacramento, raccolti et mandati in luce dal R. Nicola Laghi, da Lugano, Venice, 1599," etc.

[228] Diessenhofen, p. 155 (of Sister Adelheid von Offingen).

[229] *Vide, e.g.*, "Lestoire del Saint Graal" (The Vulgate version of the Arthurian Romance, ed. H. O. Summer, vol. i, 1909, pp. 32-35, 40-41) and "La Queste del Saint Graal," chap. xii, *ibid.*, vol. vi, 1913, pp. 189 *et seq.*

[230] A number of examples in W. Ganzenmüller's " Das Naturgefühl im Mittelalter," 1914, espec. pp. 137, 142 *et seq.*, 149-151.

[231] *Vide, e.g.*, Diessenhofen, 168, 178, Kirchberg, 142 ; Berthold von Regensburg (in the Pfeiffer edition, i, 157).

[232] *Vide* A. Graf, " Miti, legende e superstizioni del Medio Evo," vol. i, 1892, and Coll, " Il paradiso terrestro dantesco," 1897.

[233] *Vide* also ch. ii, p. 37 f.

[234] Speculum perfectionis, c. 113 (cf. also the lives of the Provençal saints of the thirteenth century — Sainte Douceline, also of the thirteenth century : " La vie de Ste Douceline," by l'Abbé Albanes, 1879, p. 58).

[235] Celano, Legenda prima, pars. 77-79.

[236] Fioretti, c. 22.

[237] *Vide, e.g.*, Speculum perfectionis, c. 113.

[238] *Ibid.*, ch. 118.

[239] " Cantico del Sole."

[240] Speculum, ch. 115.

[241] " Cantico del Sole."

[242] Speculum, ch. 116 ; cf. ch. 119.

[243] " Cantico del Sole " ; cf. Speculum, ch. 119 ; I Cel., par. 80.

[244] I Celano, par. 81.

[245] *Ibid.*, par. 80 ; II Cel., par. 165.

[246] Speculum, c. 114.

[247] II Cel., pars. 170, 171.

[248] Speculum, c. 118.

[249] I Cel., par. 80 ; cf. II Cel., par. 165.

[250] Fioretti, c. 21.

[251] *Ibid.*, c. 26.

[252] Speculum, c. 115.

[253] I Cel., par. 58 ; Fioretti, c. 18.

[254] II Cel., par. 171.

[255] *Ibid.*, par. 167.

[256] I Cel., par. 61.

[257] I Cel., par. 60.

[258] Cf. Speculum, c. 114.

[259] *Ibid.*, c. 113.

[260] Speculum, c. 118.

[261] " Cantico del Sole."

[262] Cf., *e.g.*, I Cel., pars. 77, 80 ; Speculum, c. 118.

[263] Phil. i, 21.

[264] Actus beati Francisci, . . . c. 51, pars. 9-10.

[265] Lauda, lxxxii (edition 1915 in " Scrittori d'Italia ").

[266] Other memorials of Franciscan literature speak also of the ladder of the creatures by which the soul rises to the Creator, *e.g.*,

the second " Legende " of Tomaso da Celano (par. 165), also Bonaventura in his " Itinerarium mentis ad Deum," c. 11.

[267] " Scala divini amoris," ed. De la Motte, 1902.

[268] Agnetis Blannbekin, Vita et Revelationes, c. 1.

[269] Seuse, Life, ch. ix.

[270] " Comfortable Words for Christ's Lovers," being the visions vouchsafed to Lady Julian, recluse at Norwich in 1373, ed. Rev. Dundas Harford, London, 1912, ch. iv.

[271] Chap. v.

[272] Chap. viii.

[273] Julian writes as follows concerning the relationship between the human substance in its highest purity and the divine being : " I saw no difference between God and our substance, but as it were all God ; and yet mine understanding took that our substance is in God, that is to say that God is God, and our substance is a creature in God " ; cf. Inge, " Studies of English Mystics," 1907, p. 71.

[274] Julian often used the word " sin," not only to denote the ethically evil, as, for instance, in chap. xviii, where " sin " is directly contrasted with all other pain, but also in its widest sense, to denote any evil, imperfection and pain—" all that is not good " (ch. xiii).

[275] Ch. xiii ; cf. ch. xiv.

[276] Ch. xxiii.

[277] Cf. ch. xiii, xvii, xviii.

[278] Particularly in chapters xiii, xxiii *passim.*

[279] Ch. xiv.

[280] Ch. vi.

[281] " Vita Nuova," c. 26.

"So gentle and so modest my lady seems when she saluteth others, that every tongue grows tremblingly dumb, and eyes dare not to look on her.

"She goeth her way, hearing her praises, benignly clothed in humility, and seemeth to be a thing come from heaven to earth, to show forth a miracle."—Trans. T. OKEY.

[282] C. 29.

[283] Paradiso, xxxiii, 55-57, 61-63, 82-84, 91-93, 121-123, 140-145.

> " . . . . Thenceforward, what I saw
> Was not for words to speak nor memory's self
> To stand such outrage on her skill !

> " . . . . for all the vision dies
> As 'twere away ; and yet the sense of sweet
> That sprang from it, still trickles in my heart.

> " O grace, unenvying of thy boon ! that gavest
> Boldness so earnestly to fix my ken
> On the everlasting splendour, that I look'd
> While sight was unconsumed. . . .

NOTES

" The universal form ; for that whene'er
I do but speak of it, my soul dilates
Beyond her proper self. . . .

  . . . . . .

" . . . . O speech !
How feeble and how faint art thou to give
Conception birth. Yet this, to what I saw
Is less than little. . . .

  . . . . . .

" . . . . a flash darted athwart my mind
And, in the spleen, unfolded what it sought,
Here vigour failed the towering fantasy :
But yet the will roll'd onward like a wheel
In even motion, by the Love impell'd,
That moves the sun in heaven and all the stars."

Trans. H. F. CARY.

[284] Parad., i, 1-3.

" His glory, by whose might all things are moved,
Pierces the universe, and in one part
Sheds more resplendence, elsewhere less."

Trans. H. F. CARY.

[285] Ibid., v, 8-12.

" The light eternal which to view alone
Ne'er fails to kindle love, and if aught else
Your love seduce, 'tis but that it shows
Some ill-mark'd vestige of that primal beam."

Trans. H. F. CARY.

[286] Ibid., xviii, 13-19.
[287] Cf. my essay : " The doctrine of Platonic love and beauty in the Literature of the Renaissance " (Journal of the Russian Ministry of Education, 1913, Jan. and Feb.).
[288] Obras del venerable Padre Fray Juan de la Cruz, Madrid, Tomo ii, pp. 408 passim.
[289] " . . . Il me dit que Dieu lui avait fait une grâce singulière dans sa conversion, étant encore dans le monde, âgé de 18 ans. Qu'un jour en hiver, regardant un arbre dépouillé de ses feuilles and considérant que quelque temps après ses feuilles paraîtroient de nouveau, puis des fleurs et des fruits, il reçut une haute veue de la providence et de la puissance de Dieu, qui ne s'est jamais effacié de son âme : Que cette veue le détacha entièrement du monde et lui donna un tel amour pour Dieu, qu'il ne pouvait pas dire s'il étoit augmenté depuis plus de quarante ans qu'il avait receu cette grace." Entretiens avec le F. Laurent de la Resurrection (in " Recueil de Divers Traités de Théologie Mystique " . . . Cologne, 1699), i: Entretiens, p. 46. Cf. Novalis, Fragmente vermischten Inhalts Nr. 346 (Minor)).
[290] Cherubinischer Wandersmann, i, 183.

NOTES

[291] *Ibid.*, i, 177 ; cf. also i, 185 ; ii, 109, 114, 111, 72, 90, etc.

[292] In A. v. Frankenberg's " Lebensbeschreibung Jakob Böhmes " (1651), par. 26.

[293] Jakob Böhme, " Vom Übersinnlichen Leben," 42. Cf., *e.g.*, " De Signatura Rerum," 9, 1 : " The whole outward, visible world with all its being is a sign or figure of the inward, spiritual world," *v.* also Martensen, " Jakob Böhme," 1882, p. 131.

[294] Aurora, xix, 13.

[295] " Vom Übersinnlichen Leben," 42.

[296] Aurora, x, 57.

[297] " Vom Übersinnlichen Leben," 27.

[298] Gebetbüchlein (1624), 47 (" Another prayer for Monday at noon ") ; cf. also, *e.g.*, Aurora, ii, 13, 16 : " The Holy Ghost fills all nature and is in the heart of nature and rules in the good qualities in all things " . . . " thou must here raise the mind of thy spirit to God and observe how all nature with all the forces that are in nature, also the breadth, the depth, height, heaven, earth and all that therein is, and above the heaven, is the body of God." . . . And again (xxiii, 4, 8, 9) : " . . . Thou art made out of this God and livest in Him and He giveth thee always from Himself strength, blessing, food and drink ; all thy knowledge also resteth in this God ; and when thou diest, thou wilt be buried in this God. . . . O open the eyes of thy spirit, child of man, I will always show thee the right, true, peculiar gate of the divinity. . . . Behold, this is the one true God, out of whom thou art made and in whom thou livest : When thou regardest the depths and the stars and the earth, thou seest thy God and in this same God thou livest and hast thy being also, and the same God ruleth thee also and from this same God thou hast also thy understanding and art a creature out of Him and in Him, otherwise thou wert nought." . . . But in ii : " When thou beholdest the depths, the stars, the elements, the earth, thou apprehendest with thy eyes, not the bright and radiant divinity, albeit it is certainly there present and therein ; but thou seest and apprehendest at first with thine eyes, death and then the wrath of God and the fire of Hell." Cf. also " Die hochteure Pforte " (chap. iii ; What is mystery, 13) : " Therefore we can in nowise say that God's being is something distant, having a place or position apart, for the foundation of nature and of the creation is God Himself " (cf. 14, etc.).

[299] Aurora, xxv, 20 ; cf. xxiii, 11 (quoted in the preceding note, etc.).

[300] *Vom übersinnlichen Leben*, 46. Boehme has no doctrine of the ἀποκατάστασις τῶν πάντων ; he believes in the eternity of the pains of Hell (*vide*, *e.g.*, " Forty Questions of the Soul," 32, 5 ; " Concerning the Transcendental Life," 45, etc. Cf. on this point Martensen, l.c., pp. 259 *et seq.*). For Boehme's Cosmology, *vide* also Paul Hankamer's J. Böhme, 1924.

[301] Novalis, Fragmente vermischten Inhalts, 417 (Novalis, Schriften, hrsg von J. Minor, ii, Bd. 1907, p. 310).

[302] See especially the Spiritual Songs, i, v, viii.

[303] *Vide* " Otkrovennye raskazy strannika," pp. 39-40.

[304] *Ibid.*, 93.

NOTES

[305] *Ibid.*, 31.

[306] " The Brothers Karamasov."

[307] *Ibid.*

[308] I Cor. xv, 28. It would be worth while to devote a special work to the study of the doctrine of the " Restoration of all things " among the Christian mystics. Cf. especially the ardent and inspired hopes of Julian of Norwich (l.c., chs. xiii-xvii).

[309] Matt. xxviii, 20.

[310] Matt. xviii, 20.

[311] I Cor. xi, 24.

[312] John xiv, 19 *et seq.*

[313] John vi, 54 *et seq.*

[314] Luke xxiv, 35.

[315] Cf. R. Seeberg's " The Origin of the Christian Faith," 1914, p. 10, Anm. i ; the same author's " Manual of the History of Dogma," 1922, p. 166 ; von der Goltz's " Prayer in the earliest Christian Times," 1921, p. 214 ; G. P. Wetter's " Early Christian Liturgies," 1901, p. 22, note 39. (All in German.)

[316] Acts ii, 46.

[317] I Cor. x, 16 ; xi, 29.

[318] " Didache," c. 10.

[319] I Cor. xvi, 20, 22.

[320] (Acta Thomae, c. 49.) In the Syrian text of the Acts we have a much fuller invocation first of Christ and then of the Holy Spirit (the texts, *e.g.*, in R. M. Woolley's " The Liturgy of the Primitive Church," 1910, chaps. 140-143).

[321] Greek text, *e.g.*, in Rauschen's " Florilegium patristicum," vii : Monumenta eucharistica, 1914, pp. 29-30.

[322] Greek text, *e.g.*, in Brightman's " Liturgies Eastern and Western," i, 189b, p. 21.

[323] Ethiopian text, J. S. R. Srawley's " The Early History of Liturgy," Cambr., 1913, pp. 57-58 ; R. M. Woolley's, l.c., p. 153. In this " Church Ordinance " we possess, it appears, a text originally in Greek of the Roman Hippolytos (beginning of the third century). S. A. Baumstark, " Of the Historical Development of the Liturgy " (German), 1923, p. 18.

[324] *Vide*, *e.g.*, Maltzew's " Liturgikon," 1902, pp. 921-6 ; J. H. Strawley, 205 *et seq.* ; Heiler's " Catholicism," 1923, pp. 400 *et seq.* ; Watterich's " Das Konsekrationsmoment im Heiligen Abendmahl und seine Geschichte," 1896.

[325] Brightman, 54.

[326] Ferotin's " Le libre ordinum en usage dans l'eglise wisigothique." . . . " Monumenta ecclesiae liturgica," ed. Cabrol et Leclercq, v.

[327] Wetter, l.c., p. 14.

[328] Renaudot, " Liturgiarum Orientalium Collectio," 1847 (?), i, S. 479.

[329] Cf. the Jerusalem Liturgy as described by Cyril of Jerusalem (Cath. myst., 5, 5), of the Antioch Liturgy by John Chrysostom (De poenitentia, ix, 1 ; Brightman, 47), also the Clementine and the still earlier (middle of the third or beginning of the fourth century) Liturgy

NOTES

of the so-called "Egyptian Church Ordinance" in the Ethiopian and Latin texts (the text given by, e.g., Woolley, l.c., 153-154). The "sursum corda," with the response, is already known to Cyprian. Vide Strawley, l.c., 203, 219.

[330] Brightman, 29.

[331] In the ritual of the Armenian Church the celebrants sing during the Song of the Cherubim : " Lift up your heads, O ye gates, and be ye lifted up ye everlasting doors and the King of Glory shall come in. Who is the King of Glory ? He is the Lord strong and mighty, even the Lord mighty in battle. Blessed be he that cometh in the name of the Lord ! " (Brightman, 431-432). Cf. also in the Roman Mass : " Benedictus qui venit in nomine Domini."

[332] Brightman, 254 ; cf. Walter, ii.

[333] Brightman, 434.

[334] Thus in the Syrian Liturgy of James and in the Liturgy of Nestor (vide Wetter, 16-17). In the Byzantine Liturgies the curtain is, of course, drawn back before the bringing out of the eucharistic elements for the communion of the faithful.

[335] Cf. Wetter, 75, 85.

[336] From the Syrian Liturgy of St James (Renaudot, ii, 30 ; cf. Wetter, 17). Cf. in the anaphoristic prayer of the Coptic Liturgy of St Gregory : " Aeterne Domine, Deus verus de Deo vero . . . qui manifestasti nobis mysterium hoc magnum vitae, qui constituisti chorum incorporeum inter homines : qui dedisti eis qui sunt super terram, canticum Seraphim, suscipe voces nostras cum vocibus eorum qui sunt invisibiles " (Renaudot, i, 28, 93).

[337] I, Cap. ii, 26.

[338] Justin. Dial., 117. Cf. c. 41.

[339] Ep. 63, 17. Cf. also Origenes In Jesu Nave, ii, 1.

[340] Thus Christ's Passion is represented at length, e.g., in a beautiful eucharistic prayer of the Acts of Thomas (c. 158 of the Greek text. I quote the Syrian text in Wright's translation, Apocr. Acts of the Apostles, ii, 280; cf. Woolley, l.c., 146-147) : " Thy holy Body, which was crucified for our sake, we eat, and Thy life-giving Blood, which was shed for our sake, we drink. Let Thy Body be to us for life, and Thy Blood for the remission of sins. For the gall which Thou drankest for us, let the bitterness of our enemy be taken away from us. And from Thy drinking vinegar for our sake, let our weakness be strengthened. And (for) the spit which Thou didst receive for us, let us receive Thy perfect life. And because Thou didst receive the crown of thorns for us, let us receive from Thee the crown that withereth not. And because Thou wast wrapped in a linen cloth for us, let us be girt with Thy mighty strength, which cannot be overcome. And because Thou wast buried in a new sepulchre for our mortality, let us too receive intercourse with Thee in Heaven. And as Thou didst rise, let us be raised and let us stand before Thee at the Judgment of truth."

[341] Text by Woolley, l.c., 153. " We proclaim Thy death, we acknowledge Thy resurrection." Thus the Anamnese runs already in the ancient liturgical papyrus of Der-Balyzeh (Upper Egypt), and, similarly, in the Liturgy of Mark, etc. (vide Strawley, l.c., 75,

NOTES

204). Cf. also in the canon of the Roman Mass : " Unde et memores sumus . . . Christi filii tui domini dei nostri tam beato passionis necnon et ab inferis resurrectionis, sed et in coelis resurrectionis, sed et in coelis gloriosae ascensionis."

[342] Renaudot, i, 29.

[343] Similarly also in the Clementine Liturgy (Rauschen, 156).

[344] *Vide*, *e.g.*, Renaudot, i, 45, 30, 46 ; ii, 32.

[345] Cf., *e.g.*, the homilies of John Chrysostom or of the Syrian Narsai (*v.* Connolly, " The Liturgical Homilies of Narsai ; Texts and Studies," viii, 1, Camb., 1909, pp. 3, 7 ; cf. Wetter, 53).

[346] Thus in the Liturgies of John Chrysostom and Basil the Great.

[347] Renaudot, i, 75. And after the Communion the text of the Liturgy of St Basil has it : " Quae oculus non vidit nec auris audivit nec in cor hominis ascenderunt, ea praeparasti Deus diligentibus nomen sanctum tuum et revelasti ea parvulis Ecclesiae sanctae tuae " (*ibid.*, i, 81).

[348] Renaudot, ii, 38, 40 ; cf. 32, 30, 136, etc.

[349] *Cf.*, *e.g.*, " De poenitentia," hom. ix (Migne, 49, col. 345) : "Τί ποιεις, ἄνθρωπε ; . . . οὐ, ψοβῇ, οὐκ ἐρυδριᾶς . . . τὴν φοβερὰν ὥραν ψεύστης εὑρισκόμενος ; βαβαὶ τοῦ θαύματος. Τῆς τραπέζης τῆς μυστικῆς ἐξηρτισμένος, τοῦ ἀμνοῦ τοῦ θεοῦ ὑπὲρ σοῦ σφαγιαζομένου . . . τῶν χερουβιμ περισταμένων, καὶ τῶν Σεραφὶμ ἐπταμένων, τῶν ἐξαππερύγων τὰ πρόσωπα κατακαλυπτόντων, πασῶν τῶν ἀσωμάτων δυνάμεων μετὰ τοῦ ἱερέως ὑπὲρ σου πρεσβευουσῶν, τοῦ πυρὸς τοῦ πνευματικοῦ κατερχομένου, τοῦ αἵματος ἐν τῷ κρατῆρι εἰς σὴν κάθαρσιν ἐκ τῆς ἀχράντου πλευρας κενουμένου, οὐ φοβῇ, οὐκ ἐρυδριᾷς, καὶ κατὰ ταύτην τὴν φοβερὰν ὥραν ψεύστης εὑρισκόμενος. . . ."

[350] Thus, *e.g.*, in Narsai : " . . . The priest now offers the mystery of our life, full of awe and covered with fear and great dread. . . . The awful King, mystically slain and buried and the awful watchers (angels) standing in fear in honour of their Lord ! " . . . and, again : " O ye mortals, the dread Mysteries, lo, are being consecrated by the hands of the priests : let every one be in fear and dread while they are being performed." " Bend to the ground the glance of the eye of your hearts . . . and make supplication to the God of all in this hour which is full of the trembling and great fear. Let no man dare to speak a word with his mouth ; for he that speaks oversteps, transgresses the commandment. . . . And be ye standing in stillness and fear ; for with us is that Peace which is greater than all knowledge " (*v.* Connolly, l.c., pp. 7, 11).

[351] Renaudot, ii, 584.

[352] *Ibid.*, ii, 30.

[353] John vi, 56.

[354] " Didache," c. 10.

[355] Ignat. Ephes., 13.

[356] Adv. Haeres, v, 2, 3 ; iv, 18, 5.

[357] Cyrilli, Catech. mystagog., 4, 3. Cf. also in this work (5, 12) the sanctification of the limbs of the body through the contact of the Eucharist.

[358] Athanasius, Epistolae heortasticae, ii, 14, Migne, t. 26.

[359] Bibliothek der Kirchenväter, Ausgewälte Schriften des heil. Ephräm, 1873, translated from the Syrian by Zingerie, 2 vols., p. 75.

NOTES

[360] Catech. Magn., c. 37.

[361] Cf., *e.g.*, Ambrosius (De mysteriis, 8, 47): "Ista esca quam accipis, iste panis vivus qui descendit de caelo, vitae aeternae substantium subministrat, et quicunque hunc manducaverit, non morietur in aeternum et est corpus Christi."

[362] *Vide* Th. Schermann, Ägyptische Abendmahlsliturgien . . . (Studien z. Gesch. u. Kultus des Altertums, vi, Bd. 1-2, Heft, 1912), p. 86.

[363] Rauschen, l.c., 31.

[364] And, again (the same thing): " . . . To the forgiveness of sins and to eternal resurrection." " O Bread of Life, the enjoyers of which die not . . . worthy art Thou to receive the gift, . . . that all who eat Thee die not." . . . " May this Eucharist be for your life and peace, joy and health, and the salvation of your souls and bodies," etc. (*v.* Wright, Apoc. Acts of the Apostles, ii, 180-190, 268, 290 ; Woolley, l.c., 140-147, cf. above note [8]).

[365] Srawley, l.c., 127-128.

[366] Renaudot, i, 75.

[367] " Canon " hymn 1 and 8. Similarly for the Roman Church is the Eucharist " immortalitatis alimonia " (" Postcommunio " of the 21st Thursday after Whitsuntide), " pignus salutis aeternae " (Postcomm. for Sunday after the 2nd Quadragesima), etc., quoted in Heiler's " Der Katholizismus," 1923, p. 398.

[368] 1 Cor. xi, 29 *et seq.*

[369] " Didache," c. 10. " The Holy of Holies " is the solemn cry before the giving of the Sacrament in the Byzantine Liturgy of St Basil and of St Chrysostom.

[370] Ephes. B ; Philad., 4.

[371] Apol., i, c. 65.

[372] Cf. 1 Cor. xvi, 20.

[373] Brightman, 434.

[374] *Ibid.*, 49. A detailed analysis of similar prayers in the Roman Mass is to be found in Evelyn Underhill's " The Mystic Way," 1913, pp. 344 *et seq.*

[375] Brightman, 338.

[376] Cf. Ignat. Rom., vii, 3.

[377] Liturgical papyrus of Der-Balyzeh, *v.* Schermann, l.c., 83.

[378] Liturgy of the " Ethiopian Church Ordinance."

[379] Anaphora Serapionis.

[380] Liturgy of the " Ethiopian Church Ordinance."

[381] Clem. Alex. Paed., i, 6 ; ii, 2.

[382] German translation in Maltzew's " Liturgikon," p. 215. Cf. in the " Breviarum Romanum " (Orationes ante Missam Sabbato): " . . . Panis sancte, panis vive, panis munde, qui descendisti de coelo, et das vitam mundo, veni in cor meum, et munda me ab omni inquinamento carnis et spiritus. Intra in animam meam, sana, et munda me interius et exterius. Este tutamen et continus salus animae et corporis mei. Repelle a me insidiantes mihi hostes, recedant procul a praesentia potentia tuae, ut foris et intus per te munitos, recto tramite ad tuum regnum perveniam."

[383] Ignat. Ephes., 13.

NOTES

[384] Adver. Haeres., iv, 18, 5.

[385] Adv. Haeres., v, 2, 2-3.

[386] *Ibid.*, iv, 18, 5. A very good exposition of the eucharistic doctrine of Irenaeus is given by Reuz in " Die Geschichte des Messopferbegriffs," Bd. i, 1901, pp. 179-190.

[387] Homil. 47 (translated from the Library of the Fathers of the Church, 1873, Bd. 2, p. 294).

[388] *Vide* O. Casel, " Das Gedächtnis des Herrn in der altchristliches Liturgie," 1920, pp. 9, 21-22, 27-30 ; A. Baumstark, " Die Messe im Morgenland," 1906, 24-26 ; the same author's " Vom Geschichtlichen Werden der Liturgie," 1923, pp. 13-19 ; Monumenta ecclesiae liturgica, ed. Cabrol-Leclercq, vol. i, Reliquiae liturgicae vetustissimae, 1902, pp. xxxv *et seq.*

[389] O. Casel, " Das Gedächtnis des Herrn . . .," p. 5.

[390] C. 10 ; cf. Justin. I., Apol., 13.

[391] Apok., 5, 6, 8, 12, 13. Cf., *e.g.*, Schermann's " Die altchristliche Kirchenordnung."

[392] Rev. v, 6 *et seq.*

[393] C. 33, 20. Cf., *e.g.*, O. Casel, l.c., pp. 24 *et seq.*

[394] Brightman, 50 ; cf. 85.

[395] Br., 125.

[396] Brightman, 132, 176 ; Renaudot, i, 45 (the Coptic Liturgy of St Cyril).

[397] Brightman, 413 ; cf. the prayer at the breaking of bread in the Alexandrian Liturgy of St Gregory : " After Thou hast exhaled Thy spirit, Thou hast allowed water and blood to flow from Thy side that through them the whole world might be redeemed "(Renaudot, i, 1, 108).

[398] Renaudot, ii, 18.

[399] Brightman, 514.

[400] John Chrysostom describes as follows this moment in the ancient ritual of the Antioch Church (after the consecration of the eucharistic elements) : " There lieth the propitiation for the sins of the whole world, therefore we take courage then to pray for the world and for the whole Church which is there from one end of the world to the other. And the priest approaches God and prays for the cessation of war, the suppression of revolt, for peace, for a blessing on the year, for speedy deliverance from all evils, personal and public," etc. ; cf. Cyrilli, Cat. Myst., 5, 9 ; Const. Apost., viii, 12, 40-49.

[401] Brightman, 126-128.

[402] Brightman, 167, 208 ; Renaudot, i, 8, 16-17, 30, 41, 69.

[403] Rauschen, 165.

[404] Brightman, 90.

[405] Renaudot, ii, 267, etc.

[406] Renaudot, i, 479.

[407] Brightman, 337, 409 ; cf. also in the Liturgy of Nestor—Brightman, 281.

[408] Seuse, Leben, c. ix, see above, chap. 5.

[409] Col. i, 18.

[410] Eph. ii, 14 ; Col. i, 19, 20. In a " prayer before Mass " of the

NOTES

Roman Church the Eucharist is described as " coeleste sacrificium, ubi ima summis, terrens divinis junguntur " (Missale Romanum, Praeparatio ad Missam, Foria, ii).

[411] Athanasius, Epistolae heortasticae, ii, 14 (Mi., Patr. Gr., 26).

[412] Catech. magn., c. 25.

[413] " Miscuisti, Domine, divinitatem tuam cum humanitate nostra, et humanitatem nostram cum divinitate tua ; vitam tuam, cum mortalitate nostra, et mortalitatem nostram cum vita tua ; accepisti quae nostra erant, et dedisti nobis tua, ad vitam et salutatem animarum nostrarum tibi gloria in saecula " (Renaudot, ii, 41).

[414] 2 Cor. v, 2 ; Rom. viii, 23, 22.

[415] 1 Cor. xv, 53, 54.

[416] " . . . ἐκ γὰρ θανάτου πρὸς ζωὴν και ἐκ γῆς πρὸς οὐρανὸν Χριστὸς ὁ θεὸς ἡμᾶς διεβίβασεν, ἐπινίκιον ᾄδοντας " (from the " Easter Canon " of the Eastern Church).

[417] *Vide* the beautiful and sensitive passage in Ev. Underhill's " The Mystic Way," 337. This thought appears impressively in the following prayer of an Eastern liturgy : " Bind, O Lord, Thy Majesty with our lowliness and our lowliness with Thy Majesty " (from the Ethiopian Liturgy of St Gregory of Armenia, quoted by Underhill, l.c., 362). Cf. in the Roman Mass : " . . . da nobis eius divinitatis esse consortes, qui humanitatis nostrae fieri dignatus est particeps."

[418] 1 Cor. xi, 26.

[419] " Didache," c. 10.

[420] Brightman, 515 (East Syrian Liturgy).

[421] From the Byzantine Liturgy.

PRINTED IN GREAT BRITAIN BY
THE EDINBURGH PRESS, 9 AND 11 YOUNG STREET, EDINBURGH

BOOKS FROM OUR LIST

The Modern Use of the Bible

By Dr HARRY EMERSON FOSDICK, Author of *The Meaning of Prayer*, etc. Second Edition. 6s. net.

"This is the greatest book Dr Fosdick has published, and, if I mistake not, will prove to be of the greatest service. It is so reasonable and so clearly written. It is worth its weight in gold."—*Daily Telegraph*.

A Study of the Mind of Christ

By DAVID JENKS of the Society of the Sacred Mission. 4s. 6d. net.

"The reader will be impressed by the quiet strength of the author's argument, and his spiritual insight must give this work a high place among recently published works designed to inspire intelligent and earnest devotion."—*Times Literary Supplement*.

Jeremiah and the New Covenant

By Professor W. F. LOFTHOUSE, M.A. 6s. net.

"The book ought to be widely read and carefully studied. It is popular without losing depth, and manages to convey the necessary elementary information to the uninstructed reader without being tedious to the more scholarly; moreover it is always closely in touch with the concrete realities both of the prophet's time and of our own."—*Friend*.

Was Holy Communion instituted by Jesus?

A Candid Enquiry. By Canon D. S. GUY. 6s. net.

"It is long since we have read a book with such eager pleasure. . . . In fairness of temper, in lucidity of style, in clearness of arrangement, and in convincing adequacy of knowledge it may stand as an admirable example of the qualities which a work purporting to deal with so important a question as the origin of the Eucharist ought to possess."—*Modern Churchman*.

St Paul on Trial

A new reading of the history in the Book of Acts and the Pauline Epistles. By J. IRONSIDE STILL, M.A., D.D. 7s. 6d. net.

"A piece of audacious speculation . . . whatever readers may think of the argument they will certainly learn a great deal, very freshly put, about Paul and the circumstances that led to his imprisonment."—*Christian World*.

WRITE FOR DETAILED PUBLICATION LIST